LETTER-WRITING

David James, the author of more than fifty books, here explains the principles and practice of effective letter-writing. He offers sound advice and a wide range of examples covering personal and domestic correspondence – including writing to the authorities, letters of complaint and how to apply for a job – as well as business and commercial correspondence. This book will be invaluable to all those who regard letter-writing as a tedious chore which they nevertheless have to carry out.

TEACH YOURSELF BOOKS

LETTER-WRITING

David James

TEACH YOURSELF BOOKS

Hodder and Stoughton

First published 1979
Reissued 1983
Fourth impression 1987

ISBN 0 340 32441 4

Printed and bound in Great Britain for
Hodder and Stoughton Educational,
a division of Hodder and Stoughton Ltd,
Mill Road, Dunton Green, Sevenoaks, Kent,
by Richard Clay Ltd, Bungay, Suffolk

Contents

		Page
Introduction		1
1	Before you Start	3
2	Personal Letters	19
3	Writing to the Authorities	51
4	Domestic Letters	76
5	Business Letters	95
6	Selling Abroad	127
7	Miscellaneous	137
8	Methods of Address	147
9	Abbreviations	165

Introduction

Although fashion, form and formalities in letter-writing change with surprising speed, there are certain basic rules and methods of approach that should always be followed. They apply to writing a letter for a job, a letter to a friend or a letter to the local council, and it is these rules and methods which form the basis of this book. If they are followed carefully it will be possible for a reader to write satisfactory letters on a great range of subjects, and to a wide range of people, even though he has little experience of what is common in contemporary Britain.

It should be quite clear that with letter-writing, as much as with other matters, circumstances alter cases; even the wording of a simple, though important, letter for a job will depend on a variety of matters that will vary from case to case. Yet it is here that the general principles of letter-writing will prove most helpful.

These principles are outlined in the first pages of this book and give advice on the most elementary points. They are then applied to the writing of personal, domestic and business letters. There is also a chapter discussing how to write to local authorities, to the Post Office, the police, schoolteachers and doctors. A separate chapter deals with writing business letters to foreign countries and the book concludes with advice on modes and forms of address and a lengthy list of the abbreviations which are most frequently met today.

1 Before you Start

Whatever kind of letter you are writing there are some common-sense rules that are easy to forget but will bring dividends if they are properly observed. Whether you are making an application for a job, raising a query about a holiday booking, or writing a protest to the local authority, there are some effects which you hope your letter will create in every case. You will want your letter to be read easily, and without too much effort on the part of the reader. You will want its contents to be noted seriously. And you will want to create in the mind of the reader an appreciation that you are a person whose requests, complaints, or even ordinary views, are not to be brushed aside. This last point may sound a bit pompous – and, after all, pomposity or a sense of self-importance are certainly to be avoided whenever you write a letter. Nevertheless, it is true that the flood of letters being opened every morning – and this applies not only to business letters, which are a small part of our concern, but to correspondence with a multitude of people ranging from doctors to bus companies, and from tradesmen to Members of Parliament – is steadily increasing. Unfortunately, but almost inevitably in the nature of things, not all letters will get as much attention at the receiving end as they may deserve. Those letters that do get it will not, *necessarily*, have the greatest merit. But they will, just as inevitably, be those which have impressed the reader, subconsciously perhaps, that the writer knows what he is about, and is putting down his case clearly and without fuss. And more of this impression than is usually suspected arises, quite simply, from the visual impression created when the letter is read for the first time.

Notepaper

You can write on plain, unheaded, notepaper, or on headed notepaper. A business should always have headed notepaper and even for private letters many people have their address and telephone number printed at the top. But the cost of printing is of course additional to the cost of the paper and if you write only a few letters you may not think the extra cost worth while. But always buy the best quality paper that you can afford. White or cream is, with certain exceptions, preferable to coloured.

A basic difference between the notepaper used by a business-man for business correspondence and that used for private letters is one of size, since private letters can be written on smaller sized paper. It is not necessarily wrong to use larger sizes of paper but unless there is a lot to say it is wasteful and it can also look ostentatious. In the case of self-employed people, a reasonable size of notepaper on which there is printed a simple heading containing merely an address and telephone number can be used for both private and business correspondence.

Incidentally it is worth mentioning here that conventional British paper sizes – of which the most familiar are probably quarto (8 × 11 in) and foolscap (8 × 13 in) have long been giving way to the new European sizes. These have been worked out on a complicated system – based on a rectangle having an area of one square metre – which need not concern us here. There are eleven sizes, all prefixed by the letter 'A', and the sizes most likely to concern the average letter-writer are A4 which is 210 mm by 297 mm (8.27 in by 11.69 in); A5 which is 148 mm by 210 mm (5.83 in by 8.27 in) and A6 which is 105 mm by 148 mm (4.13 in by 5.83 in). Whether you are concerned primarily with private stationery, or with business stationery which nowadays is often of the A4 size, there is a lot to be said for choosing a simple, non-flowery typeface for your address. This is a matter on which even the smallest jobbing printer is usually capable of giving very good advice. There is also a lot to be said for choosing white paper and black print, which is unlikely to offend *anyone*, and in letter-writing one of the cardinal rules is to prevent a psychological 'ugh' when the reader first starts to consider what you have to say. In some businesses – a milliners or a florists would be two good examples – there may be justifiable reason for colour, for the small device or emblem incorporated in the address, or for some other typographical touch which marks the letterheading off from everyone else's. And there are, of course, some people – the most notable examples being actors and television personalities – for whom no very clear distinction can be drawn between business and private life. Here a more flamboyant personal notepaper can be acceptable. But most of us should follow a cautious rule: use notepaper that will be treated with respect – not too strong a word when considering the varieties of subjects that have to be dealt with – by the chairman of the Local County Council and will not offend the most fastidious reader.

There are more varied methods of printing than there were even a few years ago, but the two most common are 'ordinary' printing and embossing, the latter producing raised shiny letters on the surface of the paper and being considerably more expensive than normal printing. However, there is at least one heat-treatment available from many printers which produces a result very much like embossing but at very little more cost than ordinary printing. Here again the advice to follow is that of the printer, as long as you make it clear to him that you want the end-product to be simple rather than showy.

One small matter that can be overlooked, obvious as it may seem, concerns envelopes. Make sure that they not only match your paper in tone and quality, but that your letters will go into them with two folds at the most and preferably one. A point to watch here is that old-size paper may not *quite* fit the new-size envelopes, and vice versa. So if you have old stocks of either envelopes or paper, take care!

Handwritten and typewritten letters

Next comes the choice of typing your letter or writing it, a choice not nearly as clear cut as it was only a few years ago when all business letters were typed and most private letters were written by hand. Indeed, it was once considered extremely 'bad form' to type private letters, and some of the older generation still consider it to be so. But with the spread of lightweight portable typewriters the feeling has almost died out, although there are still some occasions where the use of a typewriter would probably give the wrong impression. (Letters of condolence are a good example as would be a letter to an old friend who was about to emigrate to the other side of the world.) In fact it is a good idea to write any letter which you hope will convey a really personal sincerity to the person who reads it. On the other hand, a pen-and-ink business letter can – unless it is very carefully done – arouse a certain amount of irritation in a busy office.

Of course very many more letters are written than typed, so if your handwriting is bad and your recipient is not a long-suffering but tolerant friend, you must be certain to ensure that your letter is easily readable. In other words the handwriting must be clear and legible. This ideal can be attained by following a few simple rules, the first of which is that the letters forming the words should be neither too big nor too small. One well-known scientist who died some years ago wrote in letters only a sixteenth of an inch high and with the strokes 'above' and 'below' the line hardly any bigger; only one member of his large staff was reputed to be able to read the important letters which he wrote in this miniscule script. By contrast, a famous British politician wrote in such a large script that even a few short words stretched across the full width of the page. The happy medium is what should be aimed at. In the same way, the words should be separated by gaps of the same width, since this makes any page far more easy to read. The lines of writing should be as horizontal as possible while the letters themselves should not have the eccentric flourishes which are sometimes said to reveal character; the real aim when writing a letter is that it should be read, not that it should reveal the character of the writer, however interesting that may be.

All this helps to emphasise the obvious advantage that typing has over writing; it can, even in the case of amateur typists, be read with only minimal difficulty compared with the problem of deciphering script that is not always legible. And here one special point should be made. If you write your letters instead of typing them, and unless your handwriting is impeccably clear, do print your name in brackets underneath your signature. There seems to be some sort of inhibition against this but it can be a great relief to a reader when he finds that he does not have to decide whether the letter he has read came from 'Clark', 'Stark', 'Cleach' or 'Plant'. At the same time, it is helpful if women writers make it clear whether they are 'Mrs', 'Miss' or prefer the unrevealing 'Ms'.

Laying out your letter

Once you have the notepaper in front of you, the first thing to consider is the layout of the letter. If the paper has no printed heading – and many letters that tend to fall between the two stools of 'private' and 'business' can look very effective if written or typed on a single sheet of good quality bond typing paper – your full address (not forgetting your postal code) and telephone number is written in the top right-hand corner. Slightly below this goes the date on which you are writing. Opposite, in the top left corner (or on the left at the bottom of the page, level with your signature, if you prefer it – both are equally correct) goes the name and address of the person to whom you are writing; this is necessary with business letters, but with private letters it is not done. Once again, there are many borderline cases where only the circumstances plus commonsense can suggest whether you should put it in or leave it out.

```
Mr James Band              10 Osprey Street
Secretary                  Stunningham
'Stunningham Players'      Loamshire
52 Burton Avenue
Stunningham                Jan 2nd., 19—

Dear Mr Band,
    My wife and I have only recently settled
in Stunningham. During our previous
```

```
residence in Hopton we were active
members of the Hopton Repertory Company
and would be most grateful if you could
let us have details of membership of the
'Stunningham Players'.
                    Yours sincerely,
                    James Cartwright
```

Much the same is true of whether you write 'Mr James Band' or 'James Band, Esq.'. Although an esquire was the attendant who carried a knight's gear, the 'Esq.' was, before the Second World War, used when writing to a very wide range of people. It is still correct to write to barristers, justices of the peace, the eldest sons of knights (and *their* eldest sons) as 'Esq.' rather than 'Mr', while many professional men expect the same. But the practice is changing, very largely due to American influence and many people – bank managers being a good example – who twenty years ago would have been addressed as 'Esq.', often expect no more than 'Mr'.

When writing a business letter it is sometimes useful to put a brief, underlined indication of what the letter is about, centred on the page and roughly on a level with the opening 'Dear Sir'. It might be, for instance, Claim for cancelled hotel booking or Re: Proposed Ending of Burtonshire Bus Company Route No. 45. If you are replying to a business letter, this may have a Reference Number, in which case you can put this in the place of the identifying words above – i.e. Your Ref. No. 123. This should at least prevent your letter from floating round various uninterested departments before it finally finds its way to the right desk.

There is now the layout of the letter itself to be considered, and this will depend very largely on its length. The letter will only look best if it is well-spaced on the page, with rather more white space below the end of it than there is at the top of the page, and with a good margin at the sides. Two things in particular are to be avoided. One is writing a shortish letter with the lines close together, so that the final product has an immense area of white filling the bottom two-thirds of the paper. The other is to bring the end of your letter so close to the bottom of the paper that there is barely room left for the ending and for the signature. The first mistake can be avoided by double- or even treble-spacing the letter if you are typing it or by giving the lines an equal amount of 'air' if you are writing it by hand. In the second case just leave an inch or two of white at the foot of the page and continue on the other side.

Starting and finishing

Starting and ending a private letter is in many ways more simple than starting and ending a business letter. In writing to a neighbour you will know without much thought whether you address him as 'Dear Mr Smith', 'Dear Smith', 'Dear John Smith' or 'Dear John', these being the accepted phrases in decreasing order of formality. And an ending of 'Yours sincerely' will usually come naturally enough.

In business letters there is more scope for variety, and more for mistakes. During the last quarter-century, business letters have become – once again very largely under American influence – far less formal than they once were. Nevertheless, Britain is still basically a conservative country and when dealing with the business community it is invariably wise to err on the side of too much formality rather than too little. There is rarely need to go to the lengths of what was common before the Second World War, when 'Sir' or 'Madam', written on a single line, was the customary way of starting a letter to those whom one did not know. One says 'rarely' rather than 'never' because there can be occasions when a man's reputation as a stickler for old usages is well-known and when neither 'Dear Mr Montgomery' nor 'Dear Sir' would be as acceptable as 'Sir'. In taking such a line you do, of course, run the risk of being considered too formal, but in some cases this danger will be less than that of being considered too offhand.

'Dear Sir' or 'Dear Madam' is usually the safest way in which to start a letter to someone you have never met, unless, of course, he has one of the ranks or titles which are dealt with in Chapter Eight. An important solecism to avoid is writing, when you do not know the sex of your addressee, 'Dear Sir or Madam'. This is still sometimes used when circular letters are sent to all members of an organisation, for instance, although nowadays the form 'Dear Member' is more common. In all other cases a letter-writer who does not trouble to find out the sex of the person to whom he is writing will not get, or deserve, much attention.

Just when you should address a first letter to 'Dear Mr Smith' rather than 'Dear Sir' depends both on circumstances which include the relative positions of the writer and the person to whom he is writing. If you have spoken to Smith on the telephone, or if you have met him even once, that will be enough to permit 'Dear Mr Smith'. It is on the next stages of familiarity, 'Dear Smith', 'Dear John Smith', that care must be taken. The custom varies. But a small businessman writing to a leader of industry or a young man writing to an old one would be well advised to let any hint of familiarity come first from the other side.

Ending a letter 'Yours faithfully' or 'Yours truly' has for long been the normal conclusion during the early stages of a correspondence, with 'Yours sincerely' coming only at a later and less formal stage. However this is quickly being changed by American influence, and letters addressed to perfect strangers and ending 'Yours sincerely' are quite usual nowadays.

Drafting a letter

Whether you are writing a letter of condolence to a friend or a letter of complaint to your Member of Parliament, it is always worth while to start by making a rough draft of what you want to say. It will not only save you good paper by obviating the need to tear up a nearly-finished letter when you realise that one phrase just *has* to be changed; it will also make for a more concise and effective result. For some of us letter-writing comes easily, but although words may flow in writing to a friend, stating a case or making a forceful complaint needs careful thought and exact expression. So first work out on scrap-paper precisely what you want to say, the points you want to make, and the most telling way of putting them across. Always remember that the really important thing is to have it all clear in your own mind before you even begin the rough-drafting. A mind churning with words and phrases, but without any firm ideas to harness them to, will get you nowhere.

Some of the world's great writers have maintained that they have never put pen to paper until they had a clear idea in their heads of what they were going to say. It is unlikely that many ordinary mortals will ever achieve as much as this. Nevertheless, it is a good idea, when preparing to write a letter, to sit down and decide what the main point of the letter is to be. With the exception of any background facts that the recipient must know about in order to understand your letter, the main point should come first. There should then come any surrounding 'evidence', or similar material, followed by a brief conclusion. If you think the result sounds too abrupt and clinical, remember that a good letter-writer's motto could well follow the advice given to a public speaker: 'Stand up, speak up, and shut up.' In other words, say what is essential, but not a word more.

Making a rough draft will also enable you to weed out from your letter certain phrases which are natural and acceptable when spoken but which can be quite damaging if they appear in a formal letter. So when you read over your draft before writing or typing the final version, you must ruthlessly remove such phrases, however affectionately you feel towards them. Even the most experienced writer falls into the trap of letting such phrases slip into a rough draft, so do not worry about the need to remove them. You are in good company.

Be on your guard therefore about phrases like 'OK', 'haven't a clue', 'on the dot', 'couldn't care less', 'puts you off' and 'what the traffic will stand'. In fact be prepared to cut out all the slang expressions and colloquialisms which you might normally use in casual conversation. They can make racy reading in a newspaper or magazine article, where they are quite appropriate, but are quite out of place in a formal letter, being not only slovenly but offensive to quite a number of people. Furthermore, they are a sign of the inexperienced letter-writer, and that is not the impression you will want to create.

Not all of this applies, of course, to letters to friends and acquaintances. There you can be as free and easy as you wish. The secret of intimate personal letter-writing is naturalness, and the impression it gives of talking to the person who is reading the letter.

However, there is also the not-so-formal letter that comes midway between the formal letter and the letter to a friend. You might, for instance, be making a complaint to a tradesman whom you know; your complaint will be formal enough, but you will not want to spoil a good relationship. So in this case you have to steer a course between formality and friendliness, stating your grievance clearly and concisely, but keeping the tone of your letter friendly. In these circumstances it will be as well to leave out colloquialisms.

Returning to the formal letter, there is another warning. It is not only the slang and the colloquialisms that must be avoided, but the phrases that go to the other extreme and which are really the left-overs from a business age that is long dead. But even in the past these were the signs of a bad letter rather than a good one, despite the fact that they have continued on into the last quarter of the twentieth century. You should not write of 'your letter of the 10th inst.' but 'your letter dated the 10th of this month'. One should not 'beg for the favour of an early reply', but ask 'for a reply as soon as convenient to you' or 'as soon as possible'. 'I am desirous of' is only a more pompous way of saying 'I wish to'. Avoid saying 'This is OK by us' but also avoid saying that you 'find the aforementioned entirely in accordance with our views'. It will be better if you just say 'I approve of your idea'. People 'die' rather than 'pass away' and it is better to say that you 'do not think' rather than that you 'are not of the opinion'. It is pompous to write of 'your esteemed favour to hand' when you mean 'your letter which I have just received'; or 'enclosed please find' when you mean 'I enclose'. Another horror is 're' when what you really mean is 'about'. There are also some words which are quite suitable in one context and utterly unsuitable in another. Thus it is correct to write of 'per cent' or 'per capita' but wrong to write 'as per my letter' when what you really mean is 'as I said in my letter'. The rule should always be to use short simple phrases about which there is no doubt, rather than the more complicated and possibly ambiguous phrases: in other words, 'wash basins' rather than 'ablution facilities'.

These are examples of the stilted English which tries to give an air of importance to a simple statement and should be avoided at all cost. The simple rule is to use the plain, straightforward expression, the precise word in an economical sentence. So ask yourself, at the end of each sentence, whether you have said what you wanted to say as exactly and as simply as it can be said. You will get a lot of help in this very essential process from a book called *A Dictionary of Modern English Usage* by H. W. Fowler, published by the Oxford University Press. It has run through many editions, each one being brought up-to-date and is invaluable to those who are sufficiently interested to want to write well.

Knowing what you want to say and finding the exact words for saying it will get you over the first hurdle. Next comes the question of punctuation. A lot of people think that care over punctuation is unnecessary and tends towards 'literary' slips or at the least, tends to show too much concern with detail. That of course is nonsense. The task of punctuation is to make the writer's meaning clear, and whether you are writing a love letter, a complaint to the Post Office, or an application for a job, making yourself clear is a major consideration.

Every sentence requires a full stop at the end to show that it is completed, and many sentences require one or more commas, semi-colons or even colons. Commas should not be scattered about as though from a pepper-pot; instead, each should do a definite job which in a large majority of cases will be to indicate that there is a pause in the sentence; in other words, there would be a physical pause, to help make the meaning clear if the sentence were being read aloud; and there should be a mental pause, as it were, if the sentence is being read to oneself. The task of the comma in bringing about a pause is the reason behind most of the 'rules' which have grown up about its use. One of these rules is that when an adjective is immediately followed by one or more adjectives, a comma is always placed after each adjective except the last one. Thus one would write: 'What I am offering is a good car', 'What I am offering is a good, economical car', 'What I am offering is a good, economical, trustworthy car'. But if the succession of adjectives is interrupted by 'and', then this itself has the effect of creating a pause, and therefore you would write: 'This is a good, economical and trustworthy car.'

Sometimes the use or non-use of a comma can affect the actual meaning of a sentence. If, for instance, you write: 'I am returning your cheque, which lacks a signature' you are really saying: 'I am returning your cheque. It lacks a signature.' If, however, you leave out the comma and write: 'I am returning your cheque which lacks a signature', this means that you are returning one of many cheques, the one which lacks a signature.

One point to note is that it should always be possible to remove the words between two commas and yet leave the sentence making grammatical sense. It would thus be wrong to write: 'I told the chairman that, we all sympathise with his dilemma, but we could not support his action.' If the commas were removed the sentence would be grammatically correct but no special emphasis would be given to the fact 'that we all sympathised'. The problem is simply solved by writing: 'I told the chairman that, while we all sympathise with his dilemma, we could not support his action.'

In some cases the job done by commas can be carried out by brackets or by two dashes. These devices were more popular years ago, when sentences in most business letters, as well as some private letters, tended to be longer than they are today. A long sentence spattered with commas can be confusing, however well they are used, and it was quite common to see such sentences as 'Mr Jones (who was not very co-operative at our last meeting) seemed most anxious to help, although it is still apparent, I am afraid, that he is not very much in favour of the scheme – if, in fact, he is in favour of it at all – and that we may well face opposition in future.' Nowadays, shorter sentences are preferred and the use of both brackets and dashes has declined. To a certain extent, it is still a matter of taste. In general, however, do not use either unless you feel that it is really necessary.

Other forms of punctuation are the semi-colon and the colon.

The semi-colon is used to break up a longish sentence into more easily understood parts. Thus the head of a firm might write, 'We are going to give the staff an outing; we are going to take them down to the coast for the day; and if the idea is a success we are going to repeat it next year.' The colon is used when you have to make a statement and then follow it up with an explanation, for example, 'There were six of us present: John, Jack, James, Mary, Millicent and Miranda.' If it is used before a number of words, phrases or even paragraphs, it shows that all of these are governed by the preceding sentence, which therefore does not have to be repeated. It is customary to list the points concerned below each other. Thus you could write:

'Would you please note the following points:
(i) Whatever dates are arranged, it is essential that we should be back in London by the end of May.
(ii) The total cost of the trip must not exceed £300.
(iii) We wish the amount of train travel to be kept to the minimum.'

One punctuation mark to avoid as much as possible is the exclamation mark, certainly in business letters. In private correspondence it does not matter so much, but it should still be used with care. If you feel that an exclamation mark is necessary and that the sentence is not sufficiently emphatic without it, try re-wording the sentence. There is no rule against writing: 'You have done this entirely without my permission!!' but it is very much better to re-word the sentence as follows: 'I wish to protest most strongly against this having been done without my permission.'

Another form of punctuation about which care should be taken is the inverted comma or quotation mark, of course always used in pairs. There are three general uses for quotation marks, the most obvious being to show that the words between them are not the writer's own, but someone else's, and at the same time to emphasise their importance. Thus it would be possible to write: 'Smith says that he will not attend any more meetings, whatever the reason for their being called.' But it would be more telling to write: 'Smith says that he "will not attend any more meetings, whatever the reason for their being called".' Of course, the device must only be used when there is some obvious point to it – there would be little sense in writing 'Smith says he "has received your letter".' In fact to write the sentence that way would be to imply that while Smith had in fact received your letter there was some doubt as to whether he was going to do anything about it. Quotation marks should always be used sparingly and if it is thought useful to make a number of quotations from, for instance, a report, this may make the letter appear irritating. A better plan would then be to enclose with the letter a copy of the report, possibly with certain passages marked.

The second use of inverted commas is to show that a word or phrase is not used in its normal literal meaning. Thus you might write: 'What I am most concerned about is the "atmosphere" of the meeting.' The third use is very similar, being that of enclosing in inverted commas a phrase that is not normally used in a letter. You might, for instance, write: 'If we did this the younger members of the group would probably think that we were not "with it".' It is also sometimes the practice to put within quotation marks words that are not yet completely anglicised. 'Au pair' is an example. However, foreign words should be used with extreme caution and only where no English equivalent exists or where they have been definitely brought into the English language.

Legal implications

The final point to consider is whether the letter you have written has any legal implications. It may at first sound rather frightening to mention this in the case of 'ordinary' letters, and it is certainly true that in the vast majority of cases there is nothing whatsoever to worry about. You should, of course, have taken care not to agree to buy anything or to do anything which you are not prepared to buy or to do, and you will not sign anything that could be construed as an agreement or a contract without having given the matter proper thought. Even the most inexperienced are usually aware of the possible dangers of this.

There are, however, two other points about which many people are less aware than they should be.

The first is that of libel. The difference between slander and libel is that the first is spoken and the second is written. However, they both have one thing in common: they bring someone into 'hatred, ridicule or contempt'. Now the law of defamation, which includes both slander and libel, is an extremely complicated one and in practical terms it is almost impossible to state whether certain written words and phrases are defamatory until the Court decides the issue. To a very great extent, 'it all depends'. Anyone writing a letter containing words which could conceivably be construed as bringing someone into 'hatred, ridicule or contempt' would be well advised to omit them.

It is unlikely that you will intentionally libel anyone in a letter which you write. But it is no defence to say that you did not intend to libel. It is true that provision is made in the libel laws for what is known as fair comment on a matter of public interest. However, what is or is not a matter of public interest can be interpreted in various ways and your interpretation may be different from that of the court.

There is no reason for being unduly alarmed, but the law of libel has caught many men and women of good intent, and if you have the slightest doubt you can find it very helpful to do one thing. Put yourself in the position of the person you are writing to – or of anyone else mentioned in the letter. Then ask yourself whether, having received such a letter, you might feel that your reputation or that of anyone else had been diminished if the letter fell into someone else's hands. If there is the slightest doubt, think again.

Secondly, a point that is more likely to affect letters you receive than letters you write, there is the matter of copyright. It is far less appreciated than it should be that the legal copyright in written material belongs to – or 'resides in' as the legal phrase has it – the person who wrote the letter and *not* in the person who receives and legally owns it. There are some commonsense qualifications to this. If, for instance, you write a letter to a newspaper, it is obvious that you want the paper to publish it and although the copyright in the letter is yours you have presumably given the paper the right to print it on this occasion. Where problems may arise is in the case of letters written between neighbours or acquaintances. At some future date Mr Jones, who has received a letter from Mr Smith, may wish to publish it. But although he physically and legally owns the letter that came through his letter-box, the copyright in the letter's contents belongs to Mr Smith and if Mr Jones wishes to use it he should ask the permission of Mr Smith before doing so. The point to be made here is that if you have a letter which you believe supports your case in an argument you should consider the position carefully before using it. You can, of course, console yourself to some extent with the knowledge that inadvertent and minor infringements of copyright are unlikely to be taken very seriously. However, there are always the exceptions. Ignorance of the law is no excuse, and it is better to be safe than sorry.

There are a few other legal pitfalls to be avoided in letter-writing and they will be dealt with as the subjects are discussed later in the pages of this book. Nevertheless, it is no bad thing to look over any letter before you post it and to ask yourself one further question: have I made any promise in it, legally binding or otherwise, which will cause me worry, expense, embarrassment, or all three, if I have to fulfil it. This, perhaps, well illustrates a more general rule. Draft your letters one day, 'sleep on them', then read the drafts again, even more carefully, before putting them in the post.

Finally make sure that you enclose with the letter any documents which you have said you are enclosing. They are required when writing for a car licence, often when writing about insurance, or even when writing for information from some organisation which requires a s.a.e. (stamped addressed envelope) before you will get a reply. Check that you have, in fact, enclosed what was required.

2 Personal Letters

Most of us write more personal letters than those of any other sort, and generally these do not pose problems. However, there are some letters in this area which do need thinking about. Letters of condolence, or of congratulation on birth, engagement or marriage frequently have to be written, those of condolence being especially tricky. You will want to express your feelings of sympathy in the sincerest possible way, but in spite of this there is always an under-current of feeling telling you that nothing that is said will really help very much. Nevertheless, knowing that someone is truly sympathetic can help enormously, so the aim should be to express real sympathy without showing the effusiveness that can easily creep in. So your letter should be brief but heartfelt.

Letters of condolence

There are a few brief rules which should normally be conformed to when writing letters of condolence. They are, for instance, one of the few groups which should be written rather than typed; certainly members of the older generation can feel – unreasonably, maybe – that a typed letter is altogether too business-like and cold. Secondly, no other subject should be mentioned in the letter. Even if there are pressing matters which you want to discuss with the person you are writing to, put them in a separate letter sent in a separate envelope and, unless it cannot be avoided, post it on another day.

If you have received the first news from a newspaper 'Deaths' column, you may have found at the end of it the words: 'No letters'. If so – no letters. It usually means that the relative involved just feels that he or she is not capable of replying adequately to the numerous letters which are expected. It may – depending on circumstances – be a nice thought to wait for a month or so and then write a brief note saying how sorry you were to hear the news.

In all letters of condolence, one of the most important things is to strike the correct balance between writing too much and writing too little. Another is to get over to the recipient the real sympathy you are feeling, and the best way of doing this is to use the words of everyday life rather than the words which you may feel are 'proper' in such a letter. Thus you rigorously avoid writing about the 'sad occasion' or 'happy release'. The phrases may or may not be relevant; but don't use them.

As a warning, consider the letter which you should *not* write. It would go something like this – and, unfortunately, often does.

> Dear Jean,
>   I was honestly shocked to hear from
> Mrs Jones that your beloved sister had
> passed away. Patricia had been known to me
> for many many years and I am sure that she
> will have told you of all the good times
> we had together. I know that there is
> nothing that I can do to help you in the
> appalling situation with which you are
> faced, but I nevertheless felt that I
> should put my condolences on record.

This example includes a number of unsuitable phrases; nevertheless, any one of them can very easily creep into a letter of this kind. To start with, 'honestly', which comes out very naturally in conversation, has a slightly different effect when it is written down like this. After all, it should be taken for granted that all the feelings you express are honest; to stress it inevitably raises a subconscious suspicion. There should be no need to explain where you got the news from. Mrs Jones may be a mutual acquaintance, and while there is nothing offensive in mentioning her, there is no need to drag in a third person, brevity being the aim in this sort of letter. One should take it for granted either that the sister was 'beloved' or that Jean would not wish to admit the reverse. 'Passed away' is a relic of an age in which a 'leg' was called a 'limb' and in which a pregnant woman was 'in an interesting condition'. It should be shunned as a pious substitute for an honest fact and has been gradually disappearing for a long time. It might be relevant to mention that you had known the sister for some while, but if this is common knowledge in the family, a less heavy-handed reference is all that is needed. If there is nothing you can do to help, don't rub it in. 'Condolences' is far too formal, while putting them 'on record' does suggest that you are only writing because you feel that it is the proper thing to do.

What is called for is something briefer, such as:

```
Dear Jean,
    I was shocked to hear of the death of
Patricia, who had been a good friend of
mine for many years. Do please accept my
sympathy in your loss. If there is
anything at all which I can do to help,
I do hope that you will ask me.
```

In addition to the comparatively straightforward letters of condolence to personal friends, there are those to people not in your immediate circle but with whom you are in some kind of contact, and whose bereavement you don't want to pass un-noticed – your doctor, your bank manager or perhaps a neighbour with whom you are on nodding terms. The details of your letter will depend on how long and how well you have known the person bereaved, but in any case the letter should be briefer than that to a personal friend; something along these lines would be appropriate.

```
Dear Mr Arkwright,
    I have just learned of the death of
your wife. I am so very sorry, and I want
to offer my sincere sympathy in your loss.
```

It would, if the facts and circumstances warranted it, be fitting to add some short sentence such as 'I (we) so well remember meeting her at the Society's dinner two years ago.' But as a matter of good taste you would, in the circumstances, avoid saying: 'My wife and I . . .'.

Congratulations

To congratulate friends on the birth of a child is a happier business. All the same, as with letters of condolence it is usual to confine the contents to one subject. The joy of parenthood is not increased by the information that the price of soap-flakes is going up another 5p or that there is to be another bus strike next week. There will be no difficulty in filling up a page or two about the new arrival – is it like its mother or its father? how much does it weigh? what is it to be called? when can you come and see it? There is almost no end to the questions you can ask, and as long as you keep to the mother and the baby all is well. Just make a chatty opening and go ahead. Something on the lines of the following would be suitable.

> Dear Harry and Lorna,
>   I was delighted to see from the announcement in the local paper today that you have become happy parents. Congratulations.

Then, after the chatty questions, end the letter simply and sincerely and without fuss: 'With all the best of wishes for his (her) – and your – future.'

While the accepted formula for congratulating a couple on the birth of a son or daughter has not altered so very much during the last decade or so, the same cannot be said of congratulations on engagement or marriage. Here conventions are in a state of flux. Not so very long ago, for instance, it was soberly suggested that a woman should never be congratulated on becoming engaged, only 'felicitated' or 'wished well' since it was assumed that it was the bridegroom who had been fortunate to be accepted. So, too, congratulations on marriage itself have tended to become less formal, and the wording a good deal less stilted than it was even less than a generation back.

In sending congratulations on an engagement or a marriage, a good deal will depend on how well both parties are known to the letter-writer. It can be assumed that at least one of the two people involved will be well-known to the writer, although the second partner may be anything from an old friend to a complete stranger. To the person you know, you could write something like this:

```
Dear Pamela,
    I was so pleased to read of your
engagement and am looking forward to
meeting your fiancé soon. When are you to
be married?
                    Love from Jane.
```

A similar letter should be sent to the prospective bridegroom if he is the one you know, while if you know both of the engaged couple, the note should go as follows:

```
Dear George,
    I was happy to see the announcement that
Peggy Gray and you have become engaged.
I have known you both for a good many
years now and can think of no better
match for either of you. Do let me know
when the happy day is to be. And once
again, congratulations.
```

The one thing to be avoided, as it is to be avoided in congratulations on a marriage, is to make any reference, however light-hearted, to the past life of either of the couple. It might well be justified for a man to write to an old friend that it was high time he was settling down at last after living it up for so long. It might well be justified for one woman, in congratulating another on her engagement or her marriage, to add that she was so pleased that her friend had at last made up her mind to give up drifting and had decided that marriage was the most satisfactory relationship after all. But when the letters of congratulation are being exchanged and mulled over, neither party may be too happy at what could be read between the lines. It is, in fact, very easy for the most harmless phrases to be read the wrong way, especially when they refer to personal relationships, so here above all it is wise to heed the old piece of journalistic advice: 'When in doubt, leave out.'

Births, engagements and marriages are the most frequent events which can call for a letter of congratulation but they are by no means the only ones. If a colleague with whom you are only in touch by letter has passed a professional examination, or if his son or daughter has made a good start on a career, you may wish to send a friendly note. Here, briefness and informality should be the features. In addition, you should be careful not to suggest that you heard of the success with surprise.

```
Dear George,
   So glad to hear that you passed the
Institute's Finals with flying colours.
I saw your name on the list in the press
and felt that I had to drop you this
note, brief as it is.
               With all good wishes,
                         Yours sincerely,
```

That should be the tone rather than:

```
Dear George,
   So I see that you are successfully
through the Finals. Congratulations! I
thought you would do it, but one never
knows with examinations.
```

So, too, with congratulations to a youngster on passing examinations or getting a first job.

```
Dear Jimmie,
   I hear from your father that you're
starting as a Research Assistant at the
new laboratory next month. I know that
this is what you've always wanted, so
congratulations, and the best of luck for
lots of promotion in the future.
```

You may possibly feel inclined to add a homily about working hard and diligently, maintaining the reputation of the family, etc., etc. Don't. Advice that isn't asked for tends to be irritating anyway, and the young man is either the kind who will work hard, in which case he'll take your advice as being over-obvious, or he's the sort on whom any advice will be wasted.

Apart from the letters of congratulation sent to friends or their relatives, there is another large group which does not fall into the category of 'business', even though business acquaintances are involved. These concern the public, business or professional life of men – or women – who are only business friends but in whose life, even their personal and family life, it is appropriate to take an interest.

If an acquaintance has been appointed to the Board, promoted from master to Headmaster, or has made some similar move up the ladder, your exact response will of course depend on how well you know the person concerned. But in most cases it will be acceptable to add your congratulations to a letter dealing with other, routine, matters; and if the letter is typed a PS written in your own hand can do the job effectively. Nothing too formal is needed. 'Sincere congratulations on a well-merited honour' is enough; and, if the recipient is well-known to you, the 'step up the ladder' phrase can be used. But unless you are writing to a very old friend, avoid flippancy: 'I never thought the time would come when we would have to call you "Sir" ' may be no less than the truth, but it can easily be taken the wrong way.

Whether to write or not depends very largely on two factors – just how well you know the person concerned, and just how important the honour, appointment, or move up the ladder really is. The more important the honour, the less well you need know the recipient before you can write without seeming presumptuous.

Care needs to be taken in the case of congratulating a business acquaintance on a purely personal matter. Here the golden rule, which should only rarely be broken, is not to write at all unless the personal matter – engagement, marriage, birth of a child – has been publicly announced. You yourself may have heard the news on the business or 'old boy' network and it may in fact almost be common knowledge. Nevertheless, many men try – if not always successfully – to keep their private affairs quite separate from their business life and will therefore not welcome any unnecessary linking of the two.

One point to be noted is that it is wrong to congratulate a man, or a woman, on being made an official Patron of an organisation. It is generally assumed that it is the Patron who has conferred an honour on the organisation concerned. So there is only need for a letter if you are connected with the organisation, in which case you should write a brief note of appreciation or gratitude. It could go like this.

```
Dear .....
    I am so glad to hear that you have
become a Patron of the ..... Society. I
have supported it for very many years, so
you will understand my pleasure at hearing
of your involvement.
                        Yours sincerely,
```

Thank-you letters

What might be considered the reverse of congratulation letters are the thank-you letters which are called for from time to time in business life and more frequently in private life. If a business colleague has done a favour such as arranging an introduction to someone you wished to meet, or perhaps recommending that you should be given access to a normally 'closed' institution's library, then a brief thank-you letter is almost certainly called for. The cost of a first class stamp plus a slice of your best note-paper will top up the good-will. Quite apart from the fact that in the circumstances it is more courteous to write than to telephone, the first is likely to increase your chances of getting a favourable response if you ask for help again. Your thank-you note need only be very brief along lines such as these:

```
Dear Mr .....
    I am extremely grateful for your help in
obtaining permission for me to use the
..... Library. Thank you very much
indeed.
                        Yours sincerely,
```

In the private sector, the thank-you letter is still an agreeable courtesy if you have enjoyed a party or a meal. It is true that it is becoming more usual to make a telephone call within the next day or two but, unless the occasion was merely one in a long regular series, a brief appreciative note is the thing. And brief means brief.

```
Dear Jane,
   Thank you so much for the lovely party
on Tuesday. We enjoyed it so much and the
dinner was delicious. As always, it was
delightful to meet you all again.
                With best wishes,
                        Sincerely,
```

One point to remember here is that you should always write to the hostess, not to the host, if both have been involved.

Thank-you letters sometimes provide a valuable opportunity for teaching children how to write. If it has been little John or little Jane's birthday, he or she should be persuaded to make up a brief note of thanks for birthday presents. Just a sentence or two is enough, but these should be as legible as the child can make them without getting bored in the process. Of course the very young child will print its words, which is a laborious business at that stage of development, but a simple: 'Thank you for the present, I loved it' is enough to implement the 'thank-you' habit and, when the child can abandon printing for script, the letter-habit will have been a useful lesson in spelling.

Letters to neighbours

Next on the list of letters that have to be written are those to neighbours. Here, perhaps more than in other kinds of correspondence, care, tact, and the exercise of as much restraint as possible should be the order of the day. Whatever the subject, the chances are that you will have to see – if not talk to! – a neighbour for some considerable time, so that even if your letter involves a complaint, try to resolve matters with as little hard feeling as possible. And if you should find that you are in the wrong, admit it with good grace, however hard it may be to do so.

In general, letters to neighbours fall into one of two categories. There are those written to someone whose name you know but whom you have never spoken to, and those written to someone who is known to you, perhaps only on nodding terms, or perhaps as a more familiar acquaintance. Letters to those you have not yet met should naturally be more formal than to others, although here the respective positions of writer and addressee should not be ignored. However strongly you may feel about social differences – 'differences of social class' in the old-fashioned phrase – they still continue to exist and while this is so, you are unlikely to further your own ends by pretending that they do not. If you are writing to a professional man or a retired officer in the Services, it would be unwise to start 'Dear Willoughby' or 'Dear Mr Willoughby' even though you may hope to get on friendly terms with him eventually. 'Dear Sir' would be more appropriate in such a situation.

It is also worth noting that it always pays to take a little time and trouble finding out the correct way of addressing a person who is not in the anonymous 'Mr' category. This subject is gone into in more detail in Chapter Eight. Here it is only suggested that if you are writing to someone whom you do not know, it is a good idea to find out whether he is a Dr – not necessarily a practising doctor of medicine, of course, in which case you will probably be aware of the fact, but of some other subject – and habitually uses the 'handle'. If he is a Professor he is unlikely to welcome being called 'Dr'. And remember that whatever civilian rank a man has, any military rank comes first, however curious it can look at times. Thus, 'Captain Sir James Smith'; and, technically, 'Captain Professor Smith', although in some such awkward-sounding methods of address, the person concerned will let it be known how he does want to be addressed. If there is any chance of this, try to find out by discreet enquiry.

A letter to someone whom you do not know may be written for any one of numerous reasons, one of the most usual being that you have heard that you and a new neighbour have a mutual interest. In such a case, the following would be satisfactory:

'Dear Sir' (or, if you have good evidence that he tends to be informal and friendly 'Dear Mr James'),

```
    I have heard from our mutual
acquaintance, Mr Westerby, that you have
an interest in amateur dramatics and am
wondering whether you would care to join
the small group, the Calshot Players, of
which I am secretary. We try to arrange
local productions every six months and,
apart from this, meet every month to
discuss events in the theatre. If you are
interested perhaps you would care to come
here one evening, on some date convenient
to us both, when I could give you further
details of who we are and what we do.
If you are, so soon after your recent
move to the area, too busy to consider
devoting time to such things, please
accept my apologies for troubling you.
            With the best of wishes,
                    Yours sincerely,
```

You may, alternatively, have heard that a new neighbour comes from your own home-town, that he has Service connections the same as yours, or that you have other links in common. In all of these cases there are certain commonsense guide-lines that should be followed. First of all – and unless you really *are* certain of the circumstances – be sure to make the point about 'believing' or 'hearing' of the connection. We can all be wrong, and there is no need to start off on the wrong foot with a new neighbour by assuming that he came from Yorkshire if he came from Lancashire, or by implying to an ex-Navy man that he had seen service in the Army or the Royal Air Force. Secondly, use your discretion about such phrases as 'heard from Mr Smith'. If Mr Smith has suggested that you get in touch with your new neighbour, all well and good. If not, and if the news of your letter gets back to him, he might well feel that you were just making use of passing gossip and dragging in his name unnecessarily. Finally, remember that even if the man across the road did once have your interests, did have the same home-town or some other mutual background, he may, for any of a multitude of reasons, just not want to renew his interests now or may not want to make new friends. So always incorporate a 'get-out' clause. In other words, give your correspondent the chance of turning down your proposal without feeling churlish in any way.

A good way to end your letter would go something like this:

```
    I do realise that I am taking a liberty
in writing to you like this, and if you
are not interested I hope you will excuse
me. But in any case please accept from
me a welcome to the area.
                        Yours sincerely,
```

Letters of Complaint

Writing to neighbours who have similar interests is one of the more pleasant forms of letter-writing. But there are other, less agreeable, occasions when a letter to a neighbour is called for. This happens most frequently in the larger cities where families live in close proximity to each other and friction can arise without any deliberate intention on anyone's part. Before you start writing a letter of complaint to a neighbour it is wise to remember there are two sides to every story; that most little local troubles are finally resolved by compromise and some measure of good-will on both sides; and that although the temptation is often to 'go to law', this should be avoided except as a last resort to be used in only the most unusual situations.

Of the things likely to cause trouble, the most frequent is 'noise from the neighbours', sometimes a persistently over-loud radio, sometimes the shouts and screams of children making the noise that children do make. Many areas of Britain are now covered by local bye-laws making it possible for three or more persons to protest jointly if a neighbour is persistently producing a nuisance by noise. Such protests *can* be successful, but they should be embarked on only after personal and less heavy-

handed attempts have failed. A start could be made with a letter
along these lines:

```
Dear Mr Jones,
   I wonder if you could help my wife and
myself on a matter that has been troubling
us increasingly during the last few weeks.
We spend most of our evenings very
quietly but are reluctant to complain
about the noise from your radio which we
usually hear, more loudly than you may
realise, from about 7 o'clock until well
after midnight. I wonder if you would be
good enough to tone it down, particularly
after 10 o'clock. We do both appreciate
that in houses built as closely together
as ours, it is difficult for some
inconvenience not to be caused
occasionally, but would both be grateful
if something could be done as we are now,
quite regularly, losing a good deal of
necessary sleep.
                    Yours sincerely,
```

It would be possible, of course, to add a further line or two
about the inconvenience which you understood was being
caused to other neighbours. This would be unwise, since it is
always dangerous to drag in other people without their consent.
And you could of course refer to any noise-nuisance regulations
which might be operating in your area. However, the noisy
neighbour is hardly likely to think that he is worrying you alone,
and he is more than likely aware of any regulations. To bring up
either of these two points at this stage could well act as an
irritant and make any friendly response less likely.

In many, if not most, cases the answer to a reasonable letter
such as that suggested above will be co-operative. Only if the
reverse is the case, if you are told that your correspondent
thinks he is behaving quite reasonably, will you have to take the
next step. First it will be wise to consider whether you do, in
fact, have a justifiable complaint. Are you, perhaps, unduly

sensitive about noise? Do other neighbours feel like yourself, even if they are less ready to complain?

Depending on the answers to these questions, you could be justified in writing the following:

```
Dear Mr Jones,
    Thank you for your letter of the 7th.
I am sorry that you appear unprepared to
make your radio less of a persistent
nuisance to us. I find that a number of
residents in the street are equally
disturbed by it, and think it really
likely that you are not aware of how
loudly the sounds are heard outside your
own house. I am hoping, therefore, that
you will reconsider the situation as we
want to avoid the need for taking further
action.
                              Yours truly,
```

The last line may appear to be a little obvious. Naturally everyone wants to avoid taking further action, whether the complaint is a formal complaint to the local authorities or a request to a solicitor to send a warning letter to the noisy neighbour. Nevertheless it will be no bad thing if the neighbour is carefully warned that further action is possible. 'Carefully' is here the operative word. It is never good policy to threaten, and it is even less good if you have not thought out in some detail what the results of implementing a threat are. And of course if you are not prepared to implement it, you may find yourself in a most humiliating position. Once again, it is as well to remember that the main aim of an exchange of letters of this kind is to reach a satisfactory compromise.

If this second step fails, the next possibility is an approach to the Environmental Health Officer. He is a local government officer and you will be able to get his address from the Town Hall. It is his responsibility to investigate noise pollution and he may well be able to ease along some solution which will remove the need for that unpleasant step, 'going to the law'.

You yourself may of course be the one who receives a letter

of complaint. If so, think carefully before writing a reply. The immediate reaction of most of us when anyone complains about what we are doing is to defend ourselves strongly. But this is a time to be wary. Don't allow emotion to run away with you. Your first job is to decide whether the complaint is justified or not. If it is, don't make any bones about it. We all make mistakes and we are all thoughtless at times, and if you have been annoying your neighbours without realising it, the best thing is to admit it. Honest apologies never do any harm, so your reply should go something like this.

```
Dear Mr Turner,
    Thank you for your letter of the 17th
drawing attention to the way in which our
radio sometimes distracts you. I never
appreciated that the sound penetrated the
walls so easily. I apologise for the
inconvenience to which you have been put,
and will certainly see that the volume
is reduced in future. It is also possible
that we can help matters by putting the
set in a different part of the room. If
the noise still continues to trouble you,
please let me know and I will see what
more can be done.
                        Yours sincerely,
```

Groups and societies

Much the same commonsense considerations apply if you are thinking of starting a local group. In this case a letter to the local paper is often useful, and could run along these lines:

```
To the Editor:
Dear Sir,
    A number of acquaintances have recently
suggested that it might be possible to
start a local Rambling Club in Torbay.
The intention would be to hold a meet once
a month, each member taking it in turn to
```

```
organise a walk of a dozen or so miles
which would start within an hour's drive
from Torbay. In view of the very different
excursions which could be planned from
points within a radius of, say, 40 miles,
there would seem to be excellent scope
for such a Club which could, of course, on
occasion organise more ambitious outings.
I would be grateful if anyone interested
would get in touch with me at the above
address.
                        Yours faithfully,
```

Once such a scheme gets under way, it will be someone's job to do two things: to send out the circular letters announcing the monthly meets and to prepare the annual – or perhaps six-monthly – report of the club's activities. The first can be brief and very simple, containing only the necessary facts. It could start:

```
Dear Member,
   The Club's March meet will be held on
the 26th. It will be led by Jack Jones and
start at 10.00 a.m. in the Storrington
Market Place. Walk of about 12 miles,
mid-day break at 'The Hare and Hounds',
Westchester (bring your own sandwiches)
ending at Eastern Cross (teas available).
The 6.30 p.m. bus from Eastern Cross
arrives Storrington 7.15 p.m. Options for
tea to Jack Jones by 19 March please.
                        Yours sincerely,
```

Rules for the annual report are roughly the same. First, be clear; secondly, be concise, but remember to put at the top of the report exactly what it is, thus:

'Report of the Torbay Rambling Club
for the six months ended December 31st, 1977.'

After that should come a brief summary along these lines:

'During the six months ended December 31st, 1977, the Club held seven meets. Attendances varied from 25 in June to only 10 in November, although a record might have been established at the Christmas meet on December 28 when 24 members attended, had it not been for the appalling weather of the preceding two days. The longest walk was in July when 26 miles were covered, the shortest in October was a circuit of only 10 miles.'

After that, you can continue with as much detail as you want, taking care to avoid jokes about those who failed to complete the course, remained too long over the lunch-time pint, or who seemed to be spending too much time in the company of the ladies. However true such comments may be, they are better omitted.

One task that often falls to the writer of reports is that of inviting a lecturer to talk to the Club – or, in the case of musical or similar clubs, of inviting an artist to perform. How you should set about a potentially tricky job like this will depend very much on the fame and importance of the lecturer you are writing to and, to a lesser extent, on the status of the club concerned. But in virtually all cases the first thing will be to make discreet enquiries about one point: does the lecturer normally get paid, or is it known that he is willing to lecture for nothing because of his interest in the subject.

If you can discover only that the lecturer normally asks for a fee but are unable to find out what this usually is, there would be no harm in asking him, as long as you word your letter tactfully.

```
Dear .....
    I am arranging the winter programme of
lectures for the Torbay Rambling Club and
would be grateful to know what your fee
would be for giving us at a mutually
convenient date between September and
March a one-hour lecture dealing with your
recent walk from Calais to Rome. You
would of course be our guest at dinner and
```

we would be happy to reimburse your travel
expenses.
    Our lectures are held in the Clarendon
Hall, High Street, Sandyville, and
attendances vary between 40 and 80. The
Hall has excellent facilities for the
showing of colour slides and we would of
course be delighted if you could
illustrate your lecture.
                                    Yours

If your man is known not to ask for a fee, your first sentence
would of course be changed from 'grateful to know what your
fee would be for giving us', to 'would be grateful to know
whether you would be willing to give us. . . .'
    If the reply to the fee question brings forth a figure that is
more than you can afford, the most graceful way of letting the
lecturer know this would be a letter along these lines.

Dear Mr . . . . . ,
    Thank you for your letter of . . . . . I am
afraid that the fee you ask is more than a
small club such as ours can afford.
However, I know that our members would be
extremely interested in your experiences;
I will see therefore if we can find some
way of meeting the situation and if so
will write to you again.
                            Yours sincerely,

A response along these lines will sometimes, but probably not
often, bring about a reduction in the fee.
    When an invitation to lecture has been accepted, a further
careful letter will be required. Depending on the circumstances
it should incorporate some or all of these points.

Dear Professor,
    Thank you very much for agreeing to talk
to the Torbay Rambling Club at 8.00 p.m.
on February 3rd on your Calais to Rome
walk. We have booked a room with bath at

the Tor Hotel for the night of the 3rd and
I will meet you there at 3.00 p.m. if you
are, as may be the case, driving down from
London. If you are coming by train, I will
meet you at the station, the most
convenient train being the mid-day from
Paddington which arrives at Tor Cross
Station at 5.20 p.m.
  It occurs to me that you might like to
make a brief visit to the Clarendon Hall
on your arrival. I am certain that you
will find the facilities for projecting
your slides entirely satisfactory, but if
you have any special points to raise
please do not hesitate to telephone me at
the above number.
                          Yours sincerely,

  One point that can arise in running a local society is that of
copyright. In connection with its activities you may wish to
print, perhaps on a programme, perhaps in an advertisement,
perhaps even in an annual report, a quotation from some
published book or article. The copyright in this material will
normally be held by the publisher and you must get his permission if you wish to print what the law calls 'a substantial part'
of it. What exactly forms a substantial part is a very complex
question. A few hundred words might not be considered a substantial part of a book, but four lines from a short poem could
quite easily be construed as infringing copyright. It is unlikely
that a publisher would exact any high penalty from someone who
had inadvertently just infringed copyright, but it is equally
unlikely that an honest request will get a refusal – at the worst a
small fee may be asked for. The sort of letter to write would go
like this and be addressed to:

Copyrights Department, Messrs Blank and
Blank:
Dear Sirs,
  The Little Hanbury Theatrical Society,
on whose behalf I am writing, will later
this year be producing Barrie's 'Dear

Brutus' for three nights in the Clarendon
Hall. We are anxious to print in the
programme a 300-word extract - which I
enclose on a separate sheet - from John
Smith's critique of the play which was
published by you in 'Barrie: Man and
Master'. We would be most grateful for
your permission to do this and would of
course acknowledge the source of the
extract on the programme.
                              Yours truly,

References

A totally different kind of letter involving people who know you,
or whom you know, possibly only slightly, is that in which you
are either being asked for a reference or are yourself asking for
one. Letters of this kind are nearly always associated in the
public mind with business. This is very often so, since the
majority of letters in this category concern jobs in business
houses, stores or commerce in general. However, there are
others of a more personal kind and two examples are given
here.

John Smith, who lives in a neighbouring town and whom you
have known for some years, sends you the following:

Dear James,
    Following my last promotion our finances
are in slightly better shape and we have
decided that Phyllis is to have some
regular help in the house. There is a
shortage of suitable people, particularly
as the new factory is now offering good
rates for part-time work to young, and
not-so-young, women. However, I heard the
other day that a year or so ago, when you
and Stephanie were living here, you
employed a Mrs --. I have heard in a
roundabout way that she is available and

```
wondered what you - or more particularly
Stephanie - thought of her. Do you think
she would be suitable for us?
            With regards to you both,
                    Yours sincerely,
```

Now this is not exactly a request for a reference in the accepted sense, but it is the sort of letter which demands the same care and attention in reply as if it were.

The one thing to remember is that when you give a reference, particularly if you feel critical of the person's behaviour or abilities, you can lay yourself open to a charge of defamation if the person written about believes that he or she has been libelled. It is true that in some cases the writer may be able to claim what is called qualified privilege. But to claim this successfully the writer must be able to prove in court the truth of what he wrote, and he must be able to convince the court that it would have been wrong for him to have concealed the facts in his reference. In addition he must be able to prove that his statements were not in any way malicious. To the layman writing a reference it might seem obvious that he would be able to pass all these tests. Maybe he would. But some reference-seekers can be awkward, the law of libel is complex, and it is just as well to avoid the chances of such an entanglement if you can.

It is obvious that the problem only arises when you have something less than wholly good to say about the person concerned, and in this case you have the double task of being fair to the person who has asked for the reference and of keeping within the law. The situation is made at least slightly less difficult by one convention which is widely accepted and understood. This is that if, in writing a reference, you omit any mention of a characteristic of obvious importance, then the person you are writing about does not have it.

To take the case in point. If you had unqualified faith in Mrs — abilities you could reply something like this:

```
Dear Ronald,
    Many thanks for your letter about the
lady we still always think of as the
```

```
admirable Mrs --. In a sentence, yes, we
certainly think she would be useful to
you. Stephanie found her a really hard
worker, very anxious to please, and with
a very intelligent idea of just what was
needed of her. Also she is extremely
honest and very good-tempered. We were
both sorry when our move here made it no
longer possible for her to come in and
'do' for us regularly.
                        Yours sincerely,
```

But the position might not be quite as simple as that and if so this could be a safe but tactfully informative reply:

```
Dear Ronald,
  Many thanks for your letter about Mrs --.
Yes, we employed her for some months
before we moved from Colchester, but I
find it difficult to say whether she
would fit your particular requirements.
I can quite understand the demand that the
new works has made for local labour but
imagine that the situation will not be so
desperate when things have settled down.
                        Yours sincerely,
```

What you would not say – even if it were true – is: 'Although she was a very good worker, I am afraid that she had a persistent love of the bottle!'.

In the same way, if the Lady herself wrote to you asking for a reference you would presumably have no difficulty if she was the paragon described in the first of the above letters. If you had not been sorry when a move ended her employment something like this would be satisfactory. 'Mrs — was employed by my wife and myself for some months in 1976 and we found her work satisfactory. We were no longer able to use her services when we moved to the above address since the distance from her home was too great for her to travel to us daily.'

Holiday arrangements

Complaints to neighbours, written references, congratulations and condolences crop up intermittently in most people's lives, but there is one type of letter or, quite frequently, series of letters which come regularly every year in the lives of nearly all of us. This, or these, concern arrangements for the annual holiday. Holiday 'letters' are sometimes thought of as being mainly the postcards sent back home to tell friends or acquaintances what a wonderful time you are having – or, of course, telling them that the weather is spoiling everything! But there is more to it than that. In fact there can be quite a mass of correspondence in this section. From the moment that you send off for holiday brochures, if that's the way you do things, there are a host of minor points that can be dealt with best by a letter that is carefully thought-out rather than one which is thrown together in a hurry.

Two points should be made about every letter concerned with booking holidays – whether it is a package tour, a suite at a luxury hotel or rooms in a small seaside boarding house. The first is to give *all* the details that are required, and to repeat them in further letters even though this may at first sight seem to be completely unnecessary. Second, rigorously check the details before you actually seal the letter and put it in the post. Leaving out details about matters which you may take for granted but the recipient of your letter may not is a common cause of trouble. So is confusion about dates. It is easier than most of us realise to make a mistake about how many days there are in a month, while June and July are both popular holiday months and with hand-written letters one can easily look like the other.

This is of course one reason for typing rather than writing letters of this sort if it is at all possible – and if it is not, then for printing out the important words. Particularly important is your signature which you should print in brackets after having written it, like this: A. J. Smith. (A. J. SMITH). It is also a good reason for confirming bookings in sufficient detail. In other words, not: 'This is to confirm my recent booking', nor even: 'This is to confirm the booking which I made in my letter of May 21st.' What is required is something like this: 'This is to confirm the booking made in my letter of May 21st, for one twin-bedded room from July 8 to July 22 inclusive at the rate of £— per week inclusive of breakfast.'

Booking rooms, either at an hotel or at a boarding house, should be among the simplest of holiday matters which you will have to deal with by correspondence. However, if you are considering staying somewhere that you have never visited before, you will be well advised to ask any necessary questions in your initial letter of enquiry rather than at a later stage. So a first letter could go as follows: 'Dear Sir' (in the case of a manager at an hotel, or 'Dear Madam' if you have reason to believe that a boarding house is run by a woman).

> Could you please tell me whether you
> have accommodation for my wife, myself and
> my 4-year-old son for the fortnight from
> June 8 to June 22 inclusive? We would
> require a twin-bedded room with
> bathroom – facing the sea if possible –
> with an adjoining room for my son. We
> would also require an evening meal as well
> as breakfast and I would like to know
> whether a mid-day meal would be available
> as and when needed. Could you also please
> tell me whether dogs (in this case a
> Sealyham) can be accommodated and whether
> they are allowed in bedrooms. I would be
> grateful to hear whether you have such
> accommodation, what your rates are and
> what deposit is required. Perhaps you
> could let me know in the not too distant
> future as I am anxious to complete
> arrangements for the holiday before going
> abroad on a short business trip.
> >   Yours truly,

You should bear in mind that normally a deposit is non-recoverable. For that reason, a holiday insurance policy should be taken out – through any High Street travel agent – to cover possible loss of deposit through illness, death etc. Of course, mere change of mind would not enable a claim to be made successfully. It should also be borne in mind that if a traveller just fails to arrive he may lose not only his deposit but – should the room remain unlet – the full cost of that room less an allowance for food and electricity.

In the preliminary letter you may also want to raise one or two specific matters which are not directly concerned with accommodation. According to circumstances, the following could reasonably be mentioned. 'I am a keen fisherman and would be grateful if you could let me have details of any fishing permits required in the area.' Or: 'I am a sailing enthusiast and would be grateful if you would let me have details of any firms on the estuary (as near as possible to your hotel) from whom I could hire a boat during my stay.' You could, of course, leave such enquiries until a later date, but it would be unfortunate if you first booked your room and then found that no more fishing permits were available or that the run on boats had been such that your chances of hiring one were slight.

If the hotel is in Britain you should get a reply, if not by return then at least within a week. If you do not, you could send a brief reminder, although an hotel that is so negligent in replying to requests for accommodation may be equally negligent in other matters.

Sometimes the reply will fail to answer one or more of the questions you have raised. This may be merely the result of a slip in the rush of business. But you should not ignore the possibility that it may be a deliberate omission made in the hope that you will not press for an answer and will book the accommodation anyway. So a reply along these lines might be suitable:

Dear Sir,
    Thank you for your letter of May 17 in reply to my enquiry of May 13 asking for a twin-bedded room with bathroom for my wife and myself, and another room for my son, from June 8 to June 22 inclusive.

```
I note that you quote a rate of £65 per
week each for my wife and myself,
inclusive of breakfast and evening meal,
and of £30 per week for my son. Before
booking this accommodation I would be
grateful if you would answer the points
raised in my letter about mid-day meals
and accommodation for our dog.
                          Yours truly,
```

Most simple recommendations are also applicable to booking train tickets, or tickets for yourself and your car on one of British Rail's motor-rail services. Check the dates and time, take a copy of what you have written, and send a follow-up letter if you don't get a reply after what you consider a reasonable interval. Just how long this is will depend on circumstances, but you should remember that a very high percentage of the British holiday season is bunched into about three months and that pressure is considerable, which is one reason for booking as far ahead as possible. Here, too, remember the chances of cancellation and the advantages of insurance.

Booking your own accommodation and your own tickets is only one way of setting about organising your holiday. An increasing number of holiday-makers prefer to have the entire arrangements handled by a travel agent, particularly if they are going abroad. There are many excellent agents whose services are available wherever you live in Britain, but they can only do their jobs as well as they wish if they are given all the necessary information in the letters written by their clients. If, therefore, you want a travel agent to plan and book a tailor-made holiday for you there are certain essential points that you should put down in your letter to him. After telling him where you want to go, these are:

1. The number of people travelling in your party;
2. The ages of the children or infants included – that is, their ages at the date of departure;
3. Length of holiday and dates;
4. Preferred method of travel;

5. The type of accommodation required – self-catering, villa, apartment, hotel;
6. If hotel, whether you want medium, first or de-luxe class;
7. Whether the accommodation provided must include any special services such as the use of a swimming pool, of baby-sitters, or of sports facilities;
8. Whether you prefer the accommodation to be near your point of arrival or whether you prefer a comparatively isolated situation;
9. Whether it is essential for you to be near a sandy beach;
10. Whether you want to be within reasonable distance of a town with (i) good shopping facilities, (ii) good entertainment facilities, (iii) points of interest such as art galleries, museums or buildings of historic interest;
11. Whether you require a self-drive car for all or part of your holiday;
12. Whether you wish to be insured and whether you want the agent to help with passports, visas or any inoculations that may be necessary;
13. Whether you want a 'tailor-made' holiday or will be content with one of the 'packages' they have available;
14. And, last but by no means least, roughly how much money you are prepared to spend.

If you prefer a package holiday offered by one of the numerous reputable tour operators the most important thing, before you start putting pen to paper, is to read the small print in the brochure with extreme care. This is not because the firms that offer package holidays have any wish to trick the customer into buying less than he thinks. The reason is really far more mundane. The prices charged by many of the package holiday firms have been pared down to such remarkably low figures – in some cases with price of accommodation and air fare being less than that of the regular air fare alone – that the firms have to make it clear exactly what it is that they are offering.

If you buy a 'package' holiday from a brochure you will be required to sign the tour operator's booking form, and pay a deposit. By doing so you agree to the booking conditions as set out in that brochure, and ignorance of that fact is no defence! Amongst the conditions there will probably be a scale of cancellation fees. So check that your agent or the tour operator can provide travel insurance, and pay the premium straight away so that it covers your deposit. It is valid immediately. Do not wait until the balance is payable on the holiday.

If going to a country with which Britain has no reciprocal health arrangements, you will need high medical coverage – *particularly* for the USA and Canada. So do not stint – £5000 coverage for possible medical expenses in the USA is not excessive. If a policy seems inadequate, ring the insurers and check if you can pay an additional premium for higher cover. Be sure to declare to the insurers if you already suffer from an existing disease, such as asthma, for instance – and of course keep a copy of your letter. If you fall ill, even with a cold, before the start of your holiday, write and tell the insurers, as this is a condition of most insurance policies. If the cold turns to pneumonia and you have to cancel, the insurers may dispute liability if you have not notified them immediately of any illness, however trivial.

Finally, watch the terms of a 'package' contract, if for an overseas holiday, to see what happens if the exchange rates affect you adversely before the holiday starts. You may be asked to make up any difference, to a certain level. Alternatively, you may find a company offering a 'No Surcharge Guarantee'. In the latter case, if the rates change in your favour you will not reap any benefit, as the tour operator has gambled with you that he will bear any losses – or gains.

If you have any doubts, raise them in your initial letter of enquiry. The answers may be contained in the thick and lavishly-illustrated brochures that you will have read, but when a large selection of holidays is offered, most of them with a variety of alternatives as far as accommodation and travel times are concerned, it is all too easy to miss the information for which you are looking.

Thus it will not be unreasonable if you ask, before booking, what time the 'night flight' leaves, and what time it arrives. And what time of the day, or early morning, will you arrive at your hotel? What is really included in the 'all-in' price? Do you or, the company, pay the airport landing charge? And is your baggage handled free? And remember that words mean no more than they say, so that if an hotel is 'within sight of the sea', it would be reasonable to ask how far away it is. Remember, also, that in the world of the package tour, as elsewhere, you rarely get more than you pay for. If £150 of travel and £150 of accommodation is being offered for £200, you can hardly expect cooking of Cordon Bleu standard – even though tour operators do offer quite remarkable value for money.

Having worked your way through the brochures, asked the questions which you feel need answering, and made up your mind, you do much as you would with any other 'buying' letter. You take a copy, check the dates, and await an acknowledgment.

At this point it may sound out of place to mention the subject of complaints. Nevertheless, if you do later wish to complain about a holiday set up by a travel agent or booked through an agent with a tour operator in package form, there are a few simple points to watch.

If you have comments on a 'package' booked through an agent with a tour operator (in which case your contract will have been with the latter as principal, not with the agent), you should address a letter to the tour operator, and make two carbon copies of it. At the top of the letter give your departure date, the resort, the name of the hotel where you stayed, the length of your stay, the port, airport or station of departure; and finally the operator's booking references which you will find on his confirmation invoice, and which will enable your file to be found easily.

Next, outline the cause of your complaint. Be as objective as possible, giving facts rather than opinions. Be accurate and precise and do not extend your remarks to the experiences of other people, however strongly you may feel about them. Remember that it is *your* complaint that is being considered. Attach to your letter photocopies of any relevant receipts or notes which will support your complaint. You should include all relevant facts but should keep the letter as short as is reasonably possible. If you have taken photographs to support your case, be sure to get extra copies so that should the originals go astray, you will still have the copies.

Send the letter and one copy to the travel agent – not the tour operator to whom it is addressed – and ask him to acknowledge receipt and to forward the letter to the tour operator with his covering letter. The operator should then investigate and reply to you via the agent – not direct. This is the standard practice since it is assumed that the agent will wish to know how matters are progressing even if he is not the principal in the contract.

The number of justifiable complaints come from an extremely small percentage of the travellers who go on holiday every year, and while 'be prepared' is a good motto there is really no cause to feel doubt as you are about to set off.

However, once you have booked your holiday, there are a few things that you should prepare to do just before you go. Among the most important is arranging that your absence won't be obvious to any potential burglars. Here two letters can do a great deal to minimise the risk. One, to the firm that delivers the daily milk, need merely say: 'I would be grateful if you would stop deliveries of milk at the above address from June 4th to June 18th inclusive, and would resume deliveries as before on the morning of June 19th.' The second letter should go to your newsagent and in similar terms should cancel deliveries of the daily paper. But here you might wish to add a line or two saying, for instance: 'I do not wish to cancel my orders for "The Economist" or for "The Wimbledon Borough News" and would be glad if you would hold these in your shop until after June 18th when I will collect them personally.' If the newsagent is a one-man business you would normally write to him as 'Dear Mr Smith' rather than 'Dear Sir'.

In both cases you could of course make a telephone call instead of sending a letter, or go into the shops concerned and give the message verbally. There is, however, a great deal to be said for putting your instructions in writing. If anything goes wrong you can then produce your evidence (that is, if you have been sensible enough to keep a copy) to show that it was not you who was in the wrong. The order books of most newsagents are complicated affairs with the help of which they try to ensure that Mr Jones doesn't get Mr Smith's *Sun* and Mr Smith doesn't get Mr Jones's *The Telegraph*. Their job is complicated enough as it is, and word-of-mouth messages can complicate it still further.

It is also a good idea to inform the police that your house will be unoccupied. Once again, put it in writing – but remember that the police have their hands full enough in any case, so word the letter tactfully. Write to the local station and, before you do so, find out the name and rank of the officer in charge. Then something like this should be helpful:

```
Dear First Officer Callaghan,
    My wife and I will be taking our annual
holiday from July 1 to July 15 inclusive
and our house at 15 Burnaby Crescent will
be unoccupied for this period, although
our friend, Mrs Coates of 7 Burnaby
Crescent, will be looking in every few
days to see that all is well. I am certain
that you and your men have their hands
more than full with routine duties, as
well as with other matters, but I would
be most grateful if you could keep a
special eye on the house while I am away.
    My address from July 1 to the 15 will be
the Majestic Hotel, Rothesay, telephone
number 000-00000.
                        Yours sincerely,
```

The phrase 'special eye' is of course slang, and would not normally be acceptable in a business-type letter; but this is one of the exceptions since the phrase conveys in friendly terms what you wish to say, while a more formal expression might sound stilted.

If you are, as suggested above, lucky enough to have a helpful neighbour who will come into the house during your absence, there will be no need to arrange for correspondence to be forwarded. If not, it is possible to arrange with the Post Office to have your correspondence re-directed to your holiday address.

One final point. Before leaving for your holiday you will, of course, see that such things as water, gas and electricity are turned off – unless, that is, you have arranged for a neighbour or friend to come into the house regularly. But you should also have checked with your insurance company – or your policy – about two things. You *may* find that you are required to let the company know when your house is unoccupied for longer than a certain period. If this is so you should send the company a brief line telling them the dates between which you will be away. You are, however, rather more likely to find that cover is restricted if the premises are left *unfurnished*, the exclusions in such circumstances possibly including theft, burst pipes and malicious damage.

You may also find – and if you do it will probably be to your surprise – that your policy stipulates that you *must*, to keep within the terms of the policy, turn off the water if you leave the house for longer than a specific period. In some cases, this can be as short as a day or two!

3 Writing to the Authorities

The last ten years have for better or for worse seen an immense increase in the number of government and local authorities who influence our lives in one way or another, and with whom we have to correspond on all manner of occasions. Writing to any authority, whether it is the Water Board, the Electricity Board, the Gas Board, or the local Council, has much in common with writing most other letters: the general rules of presenting a business-like and legible letter, expressed clearly and economically, apply in this sector as in any other. There are, however, a few additional points that should be borne in mind before we go into details.

First of all, remember that with few exceptions a letter to the authorities should be formal in tone. Secondly, the letter may well have to be passed around from one office to another, and its smallest point commented on or examined in detail. So you should, even more carefully than usual, ensure that what you say is accurate, to the point, and not unnecessarily wordy. And, whatever else you do, keep a proper copy of what you have said. By 'proper' I mean a carbon copy (which you can take just as easily if you write in long-hand as if you type) or a photo-copy which you can take for a few pence on the machines at many Post Offices and Public Libraries throughout the country. You can, of course, make another, non-facsimile copy in your own hand; but if you do that, then you may later have doubts as to whether you copied the original correctly.

Since your letter, whether it is a request for information or a complaint, will be of at least a semi-official nature, you should not introduce purely personal matters into it – unless, of course, these are directly relevant to the subject you are writing about. The Secretary, the Chairman, or the Departmental Officer to whom you are writing may be known to you, but you should never end an official letter to him with any phrase such as 'I hope we shall see you at our normal reunion at the end of the month', or 'I see that your son James has now started attending the same school as our own Christopher'. Quite apart from the fact that such comments have nothing to do with the matter in hand, there can always be the suspicion that you are trying to gain preferential treatment from a friend.

Who should you write to?

At the top of most authorities' notepaper you will see an instruction such as: 'All letters to be addressed to the Director' or 'All communications to be made to the Secretary'. There is one very good reason for this request. If you write to 'W. Smith' of the Birmingham Water Board, for instance, there may well be other W. Smiths in the organisation and there can be delay before the letter arrives on the right desk. Alternatively, Mr Smith may be on holiday, or away from his office on business. Someone else may be handling the Secretary's correspondence, but a letter addressed personally to Mr Smith might well be held over until his return. In addition, there is always the possibility that your Mr Smith may have been promoted or may even have moved on to another job. In a perfect world you would of course receive a letter starting something like: 'Your letter of May 13 to Mr William Smith has been passed on to me, since I took over Mr Smith's duties as Secretary a few weeks ago . . .' In a less than perfect world, however, you may find that your unopened letter to Mr Smith has been re-addressed to him and that it has only been attended to at the right place after considerable delay.

While this practice of writing to an impersonal 'Secretary' or 'Director' is usually correct when dealing with the bigger organisations, there are sometimes exceptions – for instance when making a complaint to a gas company or a firm of manufacturers – where one man in an organisation may have the specific task of dealing with letters of this kind. In this case, finding out who he is, and writing to him directly by name, can well be the best thing to do. Unfortunately, a lot depends on the circumstances of each case – and remember that it is very often better to write to the head of a company who will pass a complaint down to his subordinate rather than to write to the subordinate himself.

These points are all parts of the larger 'Whom do I write to?' question. Here you can always find help in the local Public Library. In many, the staff is under-manned and over-worked, but despite this the reference sections of most libraries are huge quarries of information. On their shelves you will find books or booklets which give details of your local council, and others providing information about local businesses and industries. And if you cannot, for instance, find the address of the local planning authority, the chances are that the library staff will be able to help you.

There is also one other unfailing source of help. This is the network of offices run by the Citizens Advice Bureaux. There are more than 750 of these offices in England and Wales, roughly fifty of them in Scotland and between twenty and thirty in Northern Ireland. In addition there are a number of mobile offices, mainly for the convenience of those living in isolated areas. At any of these offices you can get extremely valuable advice not only on whom to write to, but on the many complicated questions that can arise when dealing with the authorities. When in doubt, have a word with them before starting.

It may sound superfluous – but is often not – to add that once you have found the name and appointment of the man you should write to, you should then make sure that you get the 'handle' to his name correct, as well as any letters which he habitually puts after his name. This is dealt with in more detail in Chapter Eight. Here it is only necessary to point out that it is, at the very least, discourteous to address Dr Jones as 'Mr' Jones. If you are in doubt about how to address someone, and this might arise in certain ambiguous cases, or when a person appears to have a foreign title, it is quite in order to make a telephone call to his secretary to get it right. The letters after a person's name must also be right, although which ones to put and which to leave out is sometimes a difficult matter to decide. For instance scientists who are able to put FRS (Fellow of the Royal Society) after their name are often happy to have all the other signs of their professional standing omitted. Others, however, may like the lot, and there was at least one eminent scientist, now dead, whose notepaper showed that he was 'FRS, FRSE, LlD, MA, BA'.

Rates and development schemes

Of the letters written to local authorities today, some of the most numerous are those dealing with the rates. Most of the rate demands sent out are prepared mechanically and it is only rarely necessary to query the figures shown on them – although it is always advisable to check them (a simple enough procedure which basically involves multiplying the rateable value of the house by the 'poundage', the number of pence in the pound which have to be paid for every pound of rateable value). However, houses that are unoccupied – and that normally means which are empty of furniture – can be rated at a lower poundage, this varying from one local authority to the next, while business premises are normally rated at a higher poundage than private houses.

Most councils now have rent rebate systems, as well as systems that enable rate-payers to pay by instalments, and if you believe you would benefit by either you have merely to write to the local authority a brief letter which would go something like this:

```
Dear Sir,
   Since my total income from all sources
is now less than (£1500) a year, I
believe that I am entitled to a rebate in
rates under the scheme which the .....
Council now operates. I would be grateful
if you would send me the necessary
application form together with any other
information which would be helpful.
                        Yours faithfully,
```

If you believe that you have a case for a reduction in your rateable value, you can make what is known as a proposal to your local Valuation Officer, who is in fact an official of the Board of Inland Revenue. Despite the popular belief that everyone connected with the rates is flinty-hearted, such proposals can succeed, and do so not infrequently. However, they must present a reasonable case, and here 'reasonable' refers to the situation as viewed by an impartial outsider. Thus it is of little use vaguely to complain that your financial situation is so bad that you want your rateable value reduced – although, as explained above, you might in such a case be eligible for a rent rebate.

The rateable value is worked out on a system that involves the cubic feet of the house, the number of rooms, the amenities, and a number of other factors. If, therefore, the amenities, or the environment, have altered since the house was last rated there may be a chance of a change. But in such a case the facts should be put down as clearly and in as much detail as possible. But exercise common-sense; there would be little point in writing: 'The noise of traffic heard in this house has now become considerable and I believe that its rateable value should be reduced.' The sort of letter which might produce results, and which would certainly be given consideration, would go something like this:

Dear Sir,
    The above house, No.15 Sykes Avenue, was given a rateable value of £500 in October, 1975. At that date no major roads passed within 300 yards of it and there was very little noise to be heard from traffic.
    In January, 1977, the section of the town by-pass linking Sycamore Street with Cedar Street was completed and since that date has been carrying a considerable – and growing – volume of traffic. This by-pass comes to within 75 yards of the rear of No.15 Sykes Avenue and the noise of its traffic can be heard in every part of the house whatever the weather

```
conditions. The noise is loud, disturbing,
and continues well into the night.
    In these circumstances I believe that
the rateable value of the house should be
decreased to bring it into line with the
new conditions created by the by-pass, and
suggest that a figure of (£450) would
reflect the present situation.
                        Yours faithfully,
```

The effect of increased traffic noise is unlikely to be disputed. Neither is the effect of fresh buildings blocking out light, or of a factory which basically alters the environment. Erection of a school, with the inevitable noise of children, will certainly worry some people, but unless the noise is genuinely excessive a complaint about children is unlikely to get too favourable a hearing.

New roads and new buildings are the most frequent causes of a change in the environment likely to affect the rateable value of a house, and you may well wish to get as much advance information as possible on such proposed changes. If, therefore, you have heard rumours of new developments, first find from your Town Hall or, failing that, from the Public Library, the name and address of the local Planning Officer. Then write to him as follows:

```
Dear Sir,
    As the owner and occupier of No.15
Sykes Avenue I have been disturbed to hear
reports that a nine-storey block of flats
is to be built on the plot of empty land
between Number 24 and Number 30
Charteris Street. As you know, Sykes
Avenue backs on to Charteris Street and
a block of this height built on the plot
would inevitably be detrimental to the
amenities of No.15 as it would cut off a
great deal of light as well as having an
overpowering effect. I would be most
grateful if you would let me know whether
this report is true.
                        Yours faithfully,
```

It is advisable in this type of correspondence to exercise a certain amount of caution in your approach. Although you may feel certain that your information is reliable, there is always the possibility of a mistake and you lose nothing by writing in guarded terms to start with. To say that you 'have heard it reported' gives you an escape route if you have been misinformed while paving the way for further letters if these are found to be necessary.

In today's complex world, even the most conscientious official may not be fully informed of what is going on, so you might receive a reply telling you that as far as he is aware there are no plans for the erection of a block of flats in your area, and that he is certain that no permission has yet been granted. You may not feel convinced; in which case you will have to extend your enquiries and do a bit more detective work. After this you may be able to follow up with something along these lines:

```
Dear Sir,
    You may remember that I wrote to you on
May 24 regarding reports that a nine-
storey block of flats was to be built on
the vacant plot of land between Number 24
and Number 30 Charteris Street, and you
replied that planning permission had not
been granted. I see from the June issue of
'Building News', a cutting from which I
enclose, that the Chairman of .....
recently announced an extension of their
interests and referred to 'an ambitious
plan for new living units in which the
company would soon be concerned south of
the High Street in Charteris Street'.
    I would be grateful to know if the
position has changed since you last
wrote to me.
                         Yours faithfully,
```

In all such letters it is essential that no accusations should be made against anyone, even by implication. You should also remember that plans for virtually all major developments legally have to be made available to the public for a certain period during which objections can be made. So get as much information as you can as soon as you can.

The Post Office

Most complaints, and requests for information, will probably be less complicated than those involved with planning. Many are likely to be concerned with the Post Office services, and here a few words of general advice can be useful. If you have a suggestion, a query or a complaint about your mail, you should write to your head postmaster. You can find out who he is by asking at your post office or by looking him up in a telephone directory under 'Post Office'. He will help you with most enquiries and problems and it will probably speed things up if, when you have, for instance, a complaint about delayed mail, you include a photocopy of the envelope concerned. If you fail to get satisfaction from the postmaster you can write to the 'watchdog' of the Post Office – the Post Office Users' National Council, whose address you will find on a notice in your local Post Office. England, Scotland, Wales and Northern Ireland, incidentally, each have separate councils.

When it comes to the telephone service, most complaints are naturally made over the telephone itself, although there is always a lot to be said for putting a complaint in writing. It should be sent to the General Manager of your local telephone area, whose boundaries you will find in the local telephone directory. Again, as a last resort, if you fail to get satisfaction from the Post Office, there is the Post Office Users' National Council.

A third Post Office service about which you may wish to write is the National Giro which provides a wide range of services for those who use it. Any letters should be sent to the Accounts Manager at National Giro, Bootle, Merseyside, GıR OAA, who will set up standing orders for payment of regular bills, arrange for copies of statements to be provided and deal with orders for cheques, transfers and pre-addressed postage paid envelopes for sending payment instructions to

Giro. Send such orders at least a week before you want delivery – and remember that, once again, the Post Office Users' National Council is there to give help if you need it.

In all dealings with the Post Office – as with most other authorities – sweet reasonableness, an attitude of more-in-sorrow-than-in-anger, will often produce results where an outspoken expression of what you felt could be less effective. You should not, therefore, write: 'I was astounded to arrive home tonight to find that a postal packet addressed to me here, and containing valuable photographs, had been tossed into the basement area of the house where it stayed for some hours in the rain before being noticed. The packet was naturally too large to be put through our small letter-box, but my wife was at home all the day and no attempt whatsoever was made to deliver the package by hand. The service provided by the Post Office is indeed becoming disgraceful in spite of its ever-increasing cost.'

Now there are a number of things wrong with such a letter. There is no reason to say that you were astounded. The fact that you are writing is enough evidence of this. There is no point in admitting that you have a letter-box too small to take packets of the sort you are presumably used to receiving. The Post Office has for years been pointing out that larger letter-boxes make the postman's job less difficult. You do not, of course, *have* to fit one, but there is no reason for pointing out that you have not done so. The claim that 'no attempt' was made may be correct. But even the postman's knock can be missed, and it would be unwise to claim that the postman had deliberately shirked his job unless you had incontrovertible evidence that this was so. As for the last sentence it is clear from your complaint that you believe the service to be disgraceful and there is no need to repeat it.

A far more civilised way of presenting your complaint would be to write something along these lines.

```
Dear Sir,
   I found on my arrival home here tonight
that a packet brought by the postman this
morning had been thrown into the
```

basement area where it remained in the
rain until being discovered some hours
later. The postman does not appear to
have knocked – my wife was in the house
all day – and I assume that he thought the
house was empty. The packet contained
valuable photographs which could have been
irreparably damaged, and I would be
grateful if you would ensure that the
same thing does not happen again.

                    Yours faithfully,

A frequent cause of 'Complaint' letters to the Post Office
concerns telephone bills. This is a subject on which opinions
vary a lot – very possibly because of the different attitudes
adopted by writers. Again, hard facts are the order of the day,
and those which you should include are illustrated by the following example.

Dear Sir,
    I have just received my telephone bill
of £80.67 for the period ended August 4th.
The previous four bills for similar
periods, photocopies of which I enclose,
were for £45.61, £31.35, £34.45 and
£43.11. The habits of my wife and myself –
the only occupants of the house – have
not changed in any way since I paid the
first of these bills, we have had no
visitors staying with us during the
period covered by the bill for £80.67,
and there is no one other than the two of
us who has had access to the telephone.
In these circumstances I would be grateful
if you would check the accounts, since it
appears that an error has been made.

                    Yours truly,

Your MP

While the Post Office Users' Council is a responsible 'Court of
Appeal' to which you can write on Post Office matters, there are

many other areas of public life in which no comparable body exists. In such cases it is often the local Member of Parliament to whom a final appeal is made if the complaint is a serious one. One result of this is that an MP's post-bag contains a fairly high percentage of letters dealing with complaints which no-one else has been able to handle satisfactorily. This means that he is not only the extremely busy man that most of us know him to be but also a man who at times becomes a little tired of sorting out problems that could, and possibly should, have been sorted out by someone else. Bear this in mind after your opening paragraph, which will probably be along the lines of: 'I am writing as a constituent of yours for the last nine years. . .'. Depending on the character of the Member concerned – and, it must be admitted, on his majority at the last election! – you might wish to say 'constituent and keen supporter', although it is of course the duty of a Member of Parliament to serve all his constituents and not merely those of his own party.

A good deal of most MPs' mail consists of complaints about the inefficiency, or alleged inefficiency, of Government Departments in dealing with such matters as pensions, old age benefits or other cases where officialdom has apparently fallen down on its job. Here the rules, as always, are simple: be brief, be clear, and give as much factual information as possible.

However, it is by no means only personal complaints about which you may feel like approaching your Member of Parliament. He should be interested in his constituency as a whole, and there are circumstances which would warrant a letter along the following lines:

```
Dear Major Smith,
   I am writing as one of your·
constituents for more than ten years on a
subject which I feel will concern you. I
refer to the general deterioration in what
I feel should be called the environmental
standards of the Bicklin Hill area of your
constituency. When I and my wife moved to
the above address in 1967, the area
consisted entirely of one-family houses
```

making up a quiet residential area. Since
then there have been considerable changes,
few of them particularly important in
themselves, but adding up to a
considerable total. The new town by-pass
which now comes to within 100 yards of the
northern edge of Bicklin Hill has
undoubtedly induced many residents to
leave this part of the area, with the
result that many of the houses have been
converted into blocks of one-room flats
which house a constantly-changing
population. The greatly increased number
of inhabitants has of course put
additional strain on the Council's already
over-worked Refuse Disposal services.
As a result some of the streets now have
an appearance that would have been
unthinkable even a few years ago. An
increasing number of the houses are empty
for longish periods and while the police –
also over-worked and under-manned – do
what they can, the situation here
certainly makes their job more difficult.
   I am afraid that this is a rather
depressing catalogue, but I do not think
that blame for the situation should be
laid entirely on the Council. It seems to
me that there are a number of causes and
that the situation is one where the
influence of our local Member of
Parliament might help to prevent it from
getting worse. After all, no-one wants
the Bicklin Hill area to deteriorate into
a slum.
                              Yours sincerely,

The police

In the above letter we have mentioned the over-worked police
once more. It is easy, therefore, to feel that any letter you may
write to the police, in creating the need for a reply, provides

them with just one more job to do. The police themselves, however, have always taken the view that the public can help them in their work. So have no hesitation in writing to them if you believe you have proper cause to do so, first finding out by telephone the name of the officer in charge. One of the more obvious reasons for a letter could produce the following:

```
Dear Inspector Wright,
   Although curtains are still hanging in
the front room of No.13 Cedar Drive, a
house which backs on to my home at the
above address, No.13 has in fact been
unoccupied for some two or three months.
I would not mention this but for the fact
that since the leaves of the creeper have
fallen it is possible to see that one of
the back kitchen windows is open. From the
little I know of the house the window
could well provide entry into the rest of
the building, while the fairly extensive
garden does give access not only to the
backs of many houses in Cedar Drive but to
those in our own road.
   I thought I should draw your attention
to the situation since the front of the
house gives virtually no indication that
it is empty.
                          Yours sincerely,
```

So, also, with abandoned cars, about which a note on the following lines might be helpful:

```
Dear Inspector Wright,
   A red Lancia, Registration Number
XXX123Z has been standing for the last
five weeks on the disused plot at the end
of the cul de sac leading from the
southern end of Cedar Avenue towards the
Common. There may be nothing sinister
about this, but the car appears to be new
and it seems rather surprising that it
```

should have been standing there so long
without - as is shown by the earth on
which it is standing - having been moved
at all. I would not mention this if I did
not know that the station is under-manned
and that your men find it impossible to
make frequent patrols of every foot of the
ground in this very scattered area.
Yours sincerely,

In most areas, the police are still responsible for traffic control, and if you have reason to believe that their services could be improved you have every right to say so – bearing in mind, as always, that they are sometimes trying to do with a dozen men the jobs for which they really need twenty. Even so, there are circumstances which could justify the following letter:

Dear Inspector Wright,
    I am writing on behalf of many parents
on the Bicklin Hill estate who have
children attending the new school at Elm
Road. As you will know this is virtually
outside the town and is, I understand,
beyond the area where the Traffic Wardens
normally operate. Most of the children
attending the school come from the
southern part of the town. There is,
however, a large contingent which comes
from the estate and who have to cross
Parkside. This has always been a busy road
and now, following the opening of the new
by-pass, is used as a short cut round the
west side of the town, by an increasing
number of heavy commercial lorries and
private cars. The nearest pedestrian
crossing is some way up the road from the
school, and while children are of course
encouraged to use it, many do not. It is
not always possible for parents to deliver
and collect the children - and those who
can do so often find themselves in

difficulties at what is generally
considered to be an extremely dangerous
stretch of road.
　　I know that you are short-staffed, but
am nevertheless asking whether it would be
possible for you to station a policeman
outside the school for about half an hour
during the morning and the afternoon when
the children are arriving and going home.
　　　　　　　　　　　　Yours sincerely,

Such a letter could, of course, have been sent – in slightly different terms – to the head of the school concerned. However, he would merely have to pass on the request to someone else, and there is no point in making unnecessary work. This is particularly true of everyone in the educational services, as well as in the health and social services. In all of these the majority of staff are not only over-worked but have to carry out a host of ancillary duties which sometimes have only slight connection with their professional skills. They will, therefore, be grateful if it is obvious that you are trying to take up as little as possible of their time.

In writing to men and women in these services it is particularly important that you should get the tone of the letter right. They are employees of the public as surely as the bank clerk is the employee of the bank, and there is therefore no need to be apologetic when asking them for information or advice. On the other hand, as pointed out above, most of them are today involved, for better or for worse, in many tasks which are only loosely connected with teaching or medicine. So remember that in most cases, while you will not be asking a favour, you will be bringing an additional and unexpected chore to the person who deals with you.

Schools and educational authorities

Of letters to the educational authorities, perhaps the simplest are those which deal with the progress – or lack of it – of a son or daughter. How you start your letter will to some extent be governed by what you know of the Headmaster or Headmistress concerned. Unless you have already met him or her it is suitable to start with 'Dear Sir' or 'Dear Madam', although 'Dear Headmaster' or 'Dear Headmistress' is also allowable. Only when you have already met him or already been in correspondence with him, would you start: 'Dear Doctor Birch'.

In such letters there is no point in beating about the bush or trying to disguise what you really want to say. Thus you would not say: 'In some ways my wife and I feel that our son John has not quite reached the levels of attainment which we had expected he would reach by the age of 12.' What would be more useful would be a letter running like this:

```
Dear Headmaster,
   My son John, who is now aged 12, has
been at St Magdalene's for three years and
my wife and I are rather disturbed by his
lack of progress in simple mathematics.
While he reads better than most boys of
his age, and appears to be extremely
well-informed on matters of general
knowledge, his lack of ability to do even
the simplest sums is rather worrying. I
have no reason to think that this is the
fault of the tuition at St Magdalene's and
am wondering whether it is due to some
inherent lack of ability; or, to put it
bluntly, to sheer lack of interest in
figures and thus to laziness in the
subject. My own feeling is that there may
be lack of interest due to his feeling
that however hard he tries, he is bound
to get his sums wrong.
   I would be most grateful if you would
tell us what we could do at home which
might help to improve his performance.
                        Yours sincerely,
```

Rather more difficult is the letter to a Headmaster in which you wish to protest about some incident at a school. Here it is useful to consider first the kind of letter that you should not write, a letter which could well go like this if it were written on the spur of the moment: 'Dear Dr Talbot, I was shocked when I came home tonight to learn that my son John arrived home from school today with a badly cut hand which was injured while he was in the school playground this morning. Although we have not taken him to the doctor – he says that he was "given some First Aid" before he left school for home – I am astounded that there was no proper supervision of the boys. I would like to hear from you at once as I intend taking the matter further.'

Now this letter includes almost every mistake that a parent could make in the circumstances, but it is not too unlike those which masters do sometimes receive. To start at the beginning, there is really no need to explain when you heard of the incident. The relevant point is that it happened. Was John's hand 'badly cut'? The fact that you have not considered it necessary to take him to the doctor suggests that this is not so. Was there really a lack of supervision in the playground? Accidents can happen anywhere and, after all, you have only heard your son's story and he is hardly an unbiassed witness. The last sentence seems a clear indication that you intend making yourself as awkward as possible even though you have only a very incomplete version of what happened.

Nevertheless, you may feel that you have genuine cause to feel worried. If so, a letter such as the following should produce results.

```
Dear Doctor Talbot,
   My son John arrived home from school
this afternoon with a long cut on his
right hand which he tells us was the
result of an accident in the school
playground. I gather that this was treated
before he left school for home and am
grateful that this was done. However, I am
rather worried that accidents of this type
can take place. I quite appreciate that
it is impossible to supervise boys in the
playground all the time but while the
```

```
injury does not appear to be serious it
could easily have been so, and my wife and
I are wondering what exactly the
circumstances were. If you could find time
to let us know, it would set our minds at
rest.
                    Yours sincerely,
```

The chances are that such a letter will bring an explanatory reply. Only if it brings none, or if it brings something along the lines of: 'I really see no need to discuss the very minor accident to which you refer', will you feel it necessary to write again. In such cases it is always a good idea to leave your correspondent a face-saving line of retreat. If you have received no reply, you can begin:

```
Dear Dr Talbot,
   I have received no reply to my letter of
March 4 (copy enclosed), but quite
appreciate that at this time of year you
will have even more work to deal with than
usual. Nevertheless, I would appreciate a
reply in the not too distant future.
                    Yours sincerely,
```

The 'copy enclosed' is always useful in such cases since it prevents the recipient of your letter pleading that the first one must have gone astray, and would you please repeat it. This may not help him in the long run, but it gives him more time!

If a Head fails to give details your reaction will depend on how far you are really determined to push the matter. But first of all, give him the chance to change his mind.

```
Dear Dr Talbot,
   I am sorry to learn from your letter of
May 7th that you feel there is no need to
give me any information on the
circumstances of my son's accident in your
school on May 4. I quite understand that
you have many calls on your time but feel
that in this case you have not fully
```

```
appreciated the implications of what has
happened. I am reluctant to take the
matter up elsewhere and hope that you will
be able to let me have some explanation of
the incident.
                         Yours sincerely,
```

This may, of course, produce another dusty answer, and if so you will have to decide how far you wish to go along the path of complaining to the local education officer and the County Education Officer.

Rather more difficult to write, but often necessary, is the letter to the local education authority when you move into a new area. You will want your child, or children, to receive the best education that the area can offer. But so will other parents and if there are not enough 'good' places to go round, a lot will depend on how you deal with the situation. As a start you should write to the Chief Education Officer with a letter that could go something like this:

```
Dear Sir,
    I shall be moving from the above house
in London into 'The Limes', Bury Street,
Tadchester, on October 15, together with
my wife and two children, John aged 11 and
Judy aged 13. John has been attending the
Winklehurst Grammar School in Ealing and
already has the following successes in
examinations. (Then run in what these
were.) Judy who has been attending the
Ealing High School, has the following
successes. (Then list them.)

    I am naturally anxious that their
education shall be continued with as
little disruption as possible and I am
hoping that it can be arranged for John
to attend the Wickenden Comprehensive
School and for Judy to attend the Sunden
Comprehensive, which I understand has a
```

```
particularly good record in the subjects
which she hopes to present for University
entrance in a few years' time.
   If it will help I shall, of course, be
glad to discuss the matter at any time and
place convenient to both of us. I am
normally very busy at the beginning of the
week, but if any of the first three days
would be more suitable for you, I will
gladly arrange my business appointments
accordingly.
                        Yours truly,
```

Doctors

It is by no means certain that doctors would like to find themselves under the heading 'Authorities', although the incorpor-
ation of most of them within the National Health Service is at
least one justification for putting them there. A letter to your
doctor does, in practice, fall into a rather special category; and,
unless you are exceptionally lucky, you will have to write one or
more of them at various intervals throughout your life, either on
your own account or on behalf of a relative or friend.

   Before suggesting ways of handling the usual run of this kind
of correspondence, it is worth mentioning a quite formal letter
that many people forget. This should be sent to your doctor if
you change your address, even though you are still living in the
same area, and should go something like this:

```
Dear Dr Jones,
   I have been your patient for the last
three years at the above address, but
shall be moving on Sept 15 to 4 Acacia
Buildings, where my telephone number will
be .... Unless I hear to the contrary, I
shall assume that you will still be
willing to provide medical services for me
at the new address. With many thanks for
your attention since I moved into the
area,
                        Yours sincerely,
```

This may sound a little curt, but as we shall see, 'the shorter the better' is a good maxim to follow. It is, incidentally, necessary to make the point about still providing service since the boundaries within which family doctors practise in any area are often complex, and even a move from one street to the next could mean that a patient had moved out of a GPs' area.

Letters to your doctor can obviously cover an enormous range of subjects; yet whatever you are writing about, all of them will almost certainly have one thing in common. They will be going to a man – or woman – who is seriously over-worked and who each day probably has to spend more time than he wishes reading reports, letters and similar material, rather than actually 'doctoring'. This is in itself a good enough reason for making sure that your letter is as brief as possible, as legible as possible, and as coherent as possible. You should remember that unless there are unusual circumstances your doctor will already have your medical history, so there will very rarely be any point in going into the details of that.

Try to put the basic facts in the first paragraph; next, go on to what is wrong, or what advice you are needing. A typical example would be this:

```
Dear Dr Jones,
    Six months ago, after discussions with
you, I began taking the oral contraceptive
.... I have now decided to stop taking
these pills and would like to know whether
I should call upon you for further advice.
To save you the trouble of replying, I
will telephone your secretary within the
next few days.
                        Yours sincerely,
```

While this is the kind of brevity which will help a busy man, all good doctors feel that their patients should be able to write to them confidentially, as a friend, without inhibitions. There may well be matters that a patient would prefer to put down in a preliminary letter before having a face-to-face talk with the doctor. If so, a longer and more discursive letter would be justified. This is particularly the case if the problem is a psychological one. In a case like this it could well help the doctor if he had the opportunity of digesting a long and possibly even rambling letter before he met the patient to discuss the problem personally.

There are, of course, an infinitely large number of variations between the 'brief' and the 'long rambling' letter. But before sitting down to write to your doctor, think for a few minutes about the question: 'What does he really want to know before he can help me?' and then write accordingly.

There are some occasions on which it is difficult to know whether a letter is preferable to a telephone call, and this is often so when advice is sought about an elderly relative. Once again, the honest answer is 'it all depends'; but if it is considered that a letter is necessary it should be written in particularly careful terms, possibly along these lines.

```
Dear Dr James,
   You will see from your records that my
father, Mr Jonathan Smith of the above
address, has had only very minor illnesses
since he became your patient nearly
twenty years ago. He has during the last
few weeks lost his appetite, appears to
have numerous 'aches and pains', and
seems to be increasingly tired after the
slightest exertion. He maintains that
there is nothing wrong with him, and his
troubles may be largely due to his age of
81. I would, however, be extremely
grateful if you could call on him so that
we could be sure that there is nothing
radically wrong. To save you the trouble
of replying I will give your secretary a
telephone call within the next few days.
                        Yours sincerely,
```

Nowadays there are many occasions on which you may want your doctor to sign a form for you. These occasions may concern absence from work, taking out an insurance policy, or the need for a note about your general health which is required for a prospective employer. In some cases it is only rather questionably part of a doctor's job to spend his time on this sort of thing, so approach him tactfully. And remember that GPs are independent contractors to the National Health Service and so are entitled to charge a fee for any services which fall outside this contract. Any letter requesting a doctor's signature should therefore also state a willingness to pay a fee for it. Something like this would be in order.

```
Dear Dr Jones,
   I would be extremely grateful if you
would sign the enclosed form dealing
with .... I would not trouble you with it
had you not been my doctor for the last
six years, and will of course be willing
to pay your fee for this.
                         Yours sincerely,
```

The clergy

While doctors rarely wish to consider themselves as among the 'Authorities', clergymen sometimes feel even more strongly that the letters written to them definitely fall into the category of 'personal'. Nevertheless, many duties that were previously carried out by clergymen – notably those of keeping an eye on the aged – have been taken over by the social services. As a result many of the topics discussed in a clergyman's post-bag do tend to bridge the gap between personal and official. There are other ways in which the practice of writing to the local vicar has changed during the last two decades; perhaps most important is the fact that the differences between the layman's world and that of the clergy have grown less and that correspondence between one and the other is therefore much less formal.

The three events about which people are most likely to write to their local vicar are births, marriages and deaths. While it is of course possible to telephone and ask for an appointment about a christening, a brief preliminary letter is courteous. The opening will be 'Dear Mr –' if the vicar is not yet known to

you personally, and 'Dear Vicar' if the reverse is the case. The
letter, varying according to circumstance, should then merely
say:

```
Dear ....,
    I am anxious that my son, Jeremy John,
who was born a week ago, should be
christened in the church attended by both
his parents and would be grateful if we
could make arrangements for this that are
mutually convenient. To save you the
trouble of replying I will give you a
telephone call within the next two days.
                        Yours sincerely,
```

A request to discuss a marriage can with one exception be
made in the same simple terms. Re-marriage of a divorced person is regarded differently not only by the various branches of
the Christian church but even by different members of the same
branch. If a divorced person is involved it is therefore expedient
to make tactful enquiries in order to avoid a rebuff. If you
decide to approach your vicar, then a letter along the following
lines would be appropriate:

```
Dear Mr Jamieson,
    I am engaged to be married to Mrs
Kingsley-Smith who is a resident of your
parish. She is anxious that we should be
married in church and I would be most
grateful if you could arrange to see us
both in the not too distant future. I
should point out that Mrs Kingsley-Smith
was divorced from her husband three years
ago.
                        Yours sincerely,
```

A more difficult kind of letter is the one called for when an
elderly person's lost interest in the Church begins to revive in
old age. A tactful letter would go along these lines:

Dear Vicar,

I must apologise for troubling you with what you may possibly regard as a rather impertinent request. However, I hope you will understand why I am writing.

My mother who is aged 75 has been bed-ridden for some months and often remarks that she would be very grateful for a visit from you. As you will no doubt know she has not been a member of your congregation for many years, but she tells me that when she first came to this area she frequently attended the services of your predecessor and that she met you on a number of Church occasions soon after the last war. I am not at all certain of her present attitude to the Church but I do know that she would very much appreciate a talk with you. One of my two sisters is always with her during the afternoons and evenings and if you could spare her some of your time – which I am quite certain always has a number of pressing demands on it – I would be genuinely grateful.

Yours sincerely,

4 Domestic Letters

Very different in some respects from personal letters to friends, and letters to authorities, are what it is easy to consider the hum-drum domestic letters that deal with the most mundane of subjects; but just as much care is needed in writing them if you are to create the effect you want.

One example which crops up increasingly in large cities occurs when two neighbours are anxious to make changes in their boundaries to provide off-street parking. With residents having to pay substantial sums to park their own cars outside their own houses, there is a great deal to be said for seeing whether the space between detached or semi-detached houses can be used for this purpose. Yet this, although a small matter in terms of pounds and pence, demands just the right approach in an opening letter.

Before any such letter is written, the following points should be carefully considered. Have you got as much information as you can get about the person to whom you are writing. A young go-ahead businessman will respond differently from an elderly retired schoolmaster. Are you putting forward merely a tentative proposal about which you want agreement in principle, or are you offering at least a partly cut-and-dried proposition? If the latter, have you done all the necessary 'home-work'?

A proposition for joint off-street parking could come about if you had bought a new semi-detached house with, on the unattached side, a four-foot six-inch wide slip-way running from the street, past your house and that of your neighbour and leading to your back gardens, in each of which there was space for a hard standing for a car or for a garage. However, between the two slip-ways, which together were nine feet wide, there was a paling fence, while across both of them there was another fence embodying a door leading into each back garden. If the fences were removed and the two slip-ways turned into one, off-street parking at the back of the houses would be available for both owners.

The first step is a simple one: find out the name and initials of the neighbour and whether or not he runs a motor-car. The next thing is a visit to the Town Hall to discover from the Planning Officer whether there are any bye-laws covering the construction of drives and garages. Most local authorities are anxious to encourage off-street parking and while there may be some points that you will have to note, the chances are that there will be no major problems as far as the Council is concerned. Nevertheless, it is probable that there will be some legal points to be considered since both you and your neighbour will have to give each other right-of-way over each other's half of the new drive. The next thing required is an estimate of what the change will cost. Once you have got that, you are in a position to write a letter which you hope will gain your neighbour's co-operation. But you will at this stage not wish to enter into detailed nego- tiations and your letter should be worded accordingly.

```
Dear Mr Bates,
    As the new owner of .... I have already
discovered the difficulty of local
parking, and I gather that the Resident's
Parking Permit, although costing £35 a
year, gives no guarantee that one is able
to park near one's own house. I imagine
that you suffer from the same
inconvenience and I am wondering whether
you would be interested in discussing
some plan whereby the slip-ways between
your house and mine might be converted
into a wider drive giving access to our
respective back gardens, and thus making
off-street parking possible. I understand
```

```
that there are no local bye-laws which
would rule this out.
    My family and I will not be moving into
our new home for several weeks as we are
having various alterations made, but I
shall be visiting the house fairly
frequently at the weekends and
occasionally in the evening.
    If the idea interests you, perhaps you
could suggest a time when it would be
convenient to discuss it.
                        Yours sincerely,
```

Your neighbour may have certain reservations, but a letter such as the above does not suggest that he should irretrievably commit himself in any way; and, as you will have intended, it leaves the way open for a discussion at which you may be able to overcome any objections he has. So you can well expect the following reply:

```
Dear Mr Lavender,
    Thank you for your letter regarding the
local parking problem and a possible
solution. I am certainly interested
although I have certain reservations: I am
not sure that I am anxious to lose a part
of the garden, even to accommodate my car,
I am not at all certain about the cost
that would be involved, or how it would
affect the value of our respective houses.
However, these are matters that we can
discuss. If you are visiting the house
next Saturday, perhaps you and your wife
would care to drop in for a cup of tea
about 4 p.m. We shall, in any case, look
forward to making the acquaintance of our
new neighbours.
                        Yours sincerely,
```

In a fairly simple case such as this, the difference between replying by return, or after the lapse of a few days, hardly arises. However, with matters which are entirely affairs of business and which have no personal element it is a good rule not to reply too hurriedly, which could involve you in something you might ultimately regret. It is true that there are cases where a writer is justified in demanding a reply within forty-eight hours, or perhaps even by return. These are very rare, however, and the recipient of any such letter will usually wonder whether his correspondent wants to rush him into a too-hasty decision. The best and most business-like way of handling such a situation is to acknowledge the letter with a non-committal reply along the lines of:

```
Dear Mr Sykes,
   Thank you for your letter of May 12.
I will let you have a considered reply
within the next few days.
                    Yours sincerely,
```

Requests for estimates

One type of letter that most of us have to write from time to time is the request for an estimate for repairs or decorations. Unfortunately for smaller jobs there is a growing practice to give only an oral estimate. In view of the time – which equals money – required to draw up and type out an estimate that may not be accepted, this is perhaps understandable, and in fact some firms nowadays make a charge for giving an estimate. However, for any sizeable job (one which is expected to cost £100 or more) it is always wise to ask for a written estimate – and what you will get from any reputable builder will not only be in writing but will give fairly full details of what he is estimating for. Nevertheless in your initial letter you should try to make it clear what the work involves. A letter merely saying: 'I would be glad if you would give me an estimate for painting the front of my house at the address above' does not give enough information. You should say, in addition, something like the following:

```
Dear Sirs,
    I would be glad if you would give me an
estimate for painting the front of my
house at the address above. I want
included in this the windows of both
storeys, the front door and the small
portion of stucco work which covers the
front of the house to the first storey.
Although the stucco work requires some
making good the house was painted four
years ago and is, as you will see on
inspection, in good condition. If
possible, I would like this work to be
carried out within the next five weeks.
                        Yours faithfully,
```

When you receive the estimate you should check it carefully to be certain of its details, and in particular the number of coats of paint which your house will be given. This is not to suggest that the builder or decorator is less than honest: merely that he may take some things for granted, that you may take some things for granted, and that your two ideas may be different.

Complaints

It is to be hoped that all goes well. But this does not always happen, and you may possibly feel that you have a cause for complaint. If so, you should bear in mind certain considerations that you should take account of in *any* letter of complaint.

One is that with such letters it is even more important than usual not to rush off something on the spur of the moment. It is sometimes urged that you should protest while in a mood of righteous indignation, but in fact nothing could be farther from the truth. If you instead follow the precept of 'counting ten' – which in this case really means doing a number of other jobs before you sit down and write – the chances are that you will cool down before you even get a draft down on paper; and in most cases, coolness usually equals effectiveness.

Certain other rules should always be followed. First of all, make quite certain of any relevant facts you are incorporating in your letter. Secondly, put down no more than the facts. Thirdly, do not make any threats, or even indirectly imply them. Fourthly, remember that the person you are writing to may not be aware of any reason for complaint until he reads your letter. Above all, keep the tone cool and reasonable. After all, you presumably want the complaint remedied and there is a far better chance of doing this if you do not infuriate your correspondent.

One other point. Before you write at all, take into account the size of the bill, if that is what you are complaining about. It is very rarely indeed a good idea to 'go to law' if there is any other alternative. However, if you feel that you have a genuine complaint about a decorating or building bill that runs into some hundreds of pounds you may feel it worth while to take the advice of a solicitor as to how you approach the firm concerned.

However, if you decide that you can handle the matter yourself, go carefully and cautiously. The letter to avoid is illustrated by the following example. 'Dear Sirs, It is only six weeks since your men finished the work of adding a bathroom to this house and already there are cracks appearing in the plaster. I told them at the time that they were doing the job in a very slapdash way and this is the result. What is more, some of the tiles you fitted at such great cost are coming away, and although I have tried there seems to be nothing I can do to fix them. The window is also jamming badly, and if someone puts their hand through it in trying to open it, the fault won't be mine. Unless all these things are put right immediately there will be serious trouble.'

This letter contains almost every example of the wrong approach. One or more such errors are often made, and while you would be unlikely to make all of them, one or two can too easily creep in. However, they can all be avoided by a little thought. 'Cracks appearing in the plaster' is a common complaint but in fact some minor settlement frequently takes place in such circumstances and while you might be justified in raising the matter this is not the way to do so. The second sentence has two errors. The writer has made an important grammatical error and implies that the cracks are the result of his reprimand and not of slap-dash workmanship. If he really wanted to make this point he should have said: 'This is the result of very slap-dash workmanship about which I spoke to the men at the time.' However, whatever your personal opinion it would be most unwise to accuse a workman of not doing his job properly. Next, it is no good complaining about the 'great cost' of the tiles since you presumably agreed to this before the work began. Nor is it wise to admit that you yourself have 'tried' to put matters right. You might, in fact, lay yourself open to charges of creating the trouble. New windows sometimes *do* jam, and while this is certainly a cause for complaint, it can probably be rectified without difficulty and is certainly no excuse for the implied threat. Finally, if by 'serious trouble' the writer means that the firm will have legal action taken against it, this is entirely the wrong way of saying so.

The correct sort of complaint should read as follows:

```
Dear Sirs,
    Cracks are now appearing in the plaster
of the bathroom which you completed at the
above address six weeks ago. I would like
to know the cause of this and also when it
will be possible for you to carry out the
further work of re-plastering which is
required. At the same time I would be glad
if your workmen would deal with a number
of the bathroom tiles which have
unaccountably come away, and with the new
window which you fitted and which is
jamming so badly that it is impossible to
open without a great deal of strenuous
effort.
    I trust that you will be able to correct
these matters without delay and that no
further action will be necessary on my
part.
                        Yours truly,
```

Similar care should be exercised in any letter of complaint, especially if it concerns that common subject, over-charging for the repair of domestic goods. It is, of course, always wise to obtain a rough estimate before taking something like a television or a lawn-mower for repair or overhaul. However it is not always easy, or even sometimes possible, for an accurate estimate to be given. It is easy, but extremely unwise, to say: 'Do whatever is necessary.' And it is natural to feel that a genuine complaint is justified if a resulting bill is very much bigger than was expected. Once again, a reasonable approach is likely to produce the best results. And, once again, give the other party a chance of remedying matters without having to eat humble pie.

The attitude to avoid is this: 'When I left my lawn-mower with you a fortnight ago I never expected that you would do so much work on it. I thought that all it needed was a new sparking plug, change of oil, etc., and I now get what I consider to be a really scandalous bill for more than £24, which I have no intention of paying.' It is obvious from the first sentence that there was no very clear agreement as to how much work would be needed on the machine, and in the circumstances the repairer would very probably be successful if he attempted to sue for the money. If you have to deal with unsatisfactory verbal agreements, you may decide either that the repairer is 'trying it on' or that he has made a genuine mis-estimate of how much time has been spent on the job. It would be extremely dangerous to imply that he was guilty of 'trying it on' and your letter, which must unfortunately be written from a position of weakness, should go something like this:

> Dear Sir,
>   Thank you for your bill for £24.50 for repairing the lawn-mower which I left with you a fortnight ago. I am wondering, however, if there has not been some error. I gather from the parts which you list under 'Material', that you felt something more than a change of oil, new sparking plug, etc. was required, but I feel that a mistake has been made under the cost of 'Labour'. I appreciate that costs are continually rising, but having had

```
comparable work recently carried out
elsewhere on a garden cultivator, I would
be glad of your comments on the bill,
which I am returning.
                        Yours truly,
```

A conciliatory reply from a repairer who had – unconsciously or not – been 'trying it on', and who did not wish to lose custom, could be along the following lines:

```
Dear Sir,
   The lawn-mower to which you refer in
your letter of June 10 did in fact need
considerably more work than you
anticipated if it was to give satisfactory
service during the coming season.
However, I am prepared to reduce the total
bill by £5 and am enclosing an amended
invoice.
                   Yours faithfully,
```

No admission has been made of over-charging and it is no doubt hoped that the customer will not only pay up but come again.

While the cost of repairing domestic equipment is one matter about which there are comparatively few safeguards – and therefore one in which you must be expected to take your own precautions – members of the public are today protected better than ever before in two somewhat similar fields: if they buy goods which are not what they are advertised to be, or if the goods are defective. Good as such protection is, however, there is here also a right way and a wrong way of straightening things out, particularly if you are eventually forced into sending a letter to get redress.

One says 'eventually' because a letter may not be necessary at all. To start with, you can take the article back to the shop where you bought it and ask for your money back if the article is not what it was advertised to be or was defective. You have no *legal* right to a replacement, the law only giving you the right to have your money back. However, if the shop offers you a replacement and you are happy to accept it, that's up to you. The right to your money back applies not only to faulty or shoddy goods but also to goods which do not match their description or were not 'fit for their purpose'.

You can also seek advice from your local Consumer Advice Centre, if there is one in your area. There are between 180 and 200 Centres in Great Britain, run by the local authorities, and their numbers are being added to all the time. The staff at the Centre will be able to explain the latest rules and regulations which, while giving the consumer increased protection, are sometimes considered rather complicated. Incidentally, it is worth mentioning that you should not write to the national Consumers Association unless you subscribe to their Personal Service scheme (£20 a year at present) since they are unable to deal with complaints from non-subscribers much as they would like to.

Whether your first step should be to go back to the shop or to visit the Centre will depend on the complexity of the case, the attitude which from past experience you can expect the shop to take up, the amount of money involved, and whether or not you feel that a genuine mistake has been made. Some Consumer Advice Centres will not intervene *until* you have been to the shop, although they will tell you what your rights are.

Only after you have done your best at the shop should you put your complaint in writing. If you bought the goods for cash you should write to the supplier, which in most cases will be the shop; if you bought them on hire Purchase you should write to the finance company involved. In either case, you should write to 'the man at the top', the chairman or managing director, and if possible you should write to him by name. Your letter should start by putting down the facts simply and accurately. Next you should describe what went wrong; alternatively, if the article is not defective but different from its description, you would have to point this out. There should then follow what is in some ways the most important part of the letter – asking for return of the price paid. Do not forget to keep a copy, and send it by recorded delivery.

Your letter might go like this:

```
Dear Sir,
   On March 15, 19—, I bought a Mark II
..... refrigerator from ..... at a cost
of £340. Within forty-eight hours of
installation, the refrigerator ceased
to operate, and I understand from the
electrician who came to inspect the
machine that the trouble is due to a
faulty motor which will have to be
replaced. Your firm, Messrs. ..... have
refused to do this.
   I understand that the transaction is
covered by the Sale of Goods Act (1893) as
updated by the Supply of Goods (Implied
Terms) Act, 1973, and am looking to your
company for a return of the price paid
within 14 days.
                              Yours truly,
```

The time given to the vendor is a matter for the buyer to choose but 14 days is considered reasonable. If this first letter fails to bring a satisfactory reply a reminder such as the following should be sent.

```
Dear Sir,
   I have had no reply to my letter of
May 4 (copy enclosed) dealing with the
purchase of a Mark II ..... Refrigerator
from ..... and would be glad of a reply
without further delay, or I may have to
consider legal action.
                              Yours truly,
```

If this produces no result you can then employ a solicitor to take the matter to the County Court, although before doing so you would be well advised to consult the Consumer Advice Centre again; or, if none is available, some body such as the Citizens' Advice Bureau. The reason is that if a claim is made in the County Court under the 'less-than-£100' procedure you will not get your costs back even if you win.

Insurance claims

Making a claim of any sort is always a tricky operation, and this is so even if it is being made from a strong position as with an Insurance claim. Here there is one cardinal rule, whether the claim follows a burglary, storm damage to your house or, for that matter, any other incident against which it is possible to insure; this rule is: 'Read the insurance policy before you start to make the claim.' You should have done this when taking out the policy, but it is surprising how many people fail to do so. Do so now, then consider carefully before making your claim. The most obvious mistake would be to claim for something that is not covered by the policy, or is perhaps even specifically excluded. This is not the only thing to avoid. Under some policies, the holder pays the first £20, £30 or £40 of any claim, and under others he pays a certain percentage of the claim. Now it is clear that if you have sustained £20 of damage to the roof of a house and have to pay the first £30 of any claim, there is no point in making one, particularly as many insurance companies operate a system which provides free cover to non-claimants once in every so many years. In the case of small losses, you should therefore consider very carefully whether it is worth making a claim at all.

Assuming that your policy covers the incident and that you intend to make a claim it is worth while telephoning the insurer to discover whether or not there is need for you to complete a claim form. If so, you may feel that there is no need to write a letter at all. Assuming, however, that this is not so, and that a letter is necessary, write it without delay after the event. And remember that while you should put in all the relevant details, there is no point in putting in more than that.

If the damage has been caused by storm there is no point in discussing how dreadful it was; and if you have received an estimate for the work to be done – as you should – the insurers will not be interested in your comments on the high cost of labour. The following should be sufficient:

> Dear Sirs,
>   I wish to make a claim under my Policy
> No. 1234/567 for damage caused to the roof
> of this house during the storm on the
> night of September 3/4. The high winds
> lifted the tiles at the north-east corner
> of the roof, shifting them and allowing in
> the torrential rain that accompanied the
> wind. As a result, much of the plaster
> ceiling in one bedroom has collapsed, and
> it appears from inspection by a local
> builder that most of the ceiling will have
> to be replastered. The builder, Mr .....
> of ..... estimates that the cost of this
> will be £105.
>   I also wish to make a claim under
> Policy No. 123333/5746 for damage to the
> carpet and bedding in the room, some of
> which can be cleaned but some of which
> will have to be replaced. I estimate the
> cost of this to be £35.
>   A time for inspecting the damage can be
> arranged either by telephoning my wife at
> the above address or by telephoning me at
> my office number of .....
> Yours truly,

A more difficult kind of insurance letter is the one which must be written following a motor car accident. It is notorious that six honest eye-witnesses can give six contradictory accounts of the same accident, and it is most important that in writing to your insurance company you should be as accurate as possible and should strictly separate fact from opinion. First, what not to do. A bad letter would run as follows: 'Driving into London along Knightsbridge two days ago a car some way ahead of me suddenly turned round, without making any signals at all, trying to make a U-turn. I naturally ran into it and the driver blamed me for not taking care, although it was of course entirely his own fault. He says he is Mr John Jones of .... and I think it absolutely scandalous that he should be driving at all and causing accidents of this sort. His car was hardly damaged but my near-side wing is stove in, the headlamp wrecked and I should think the car would also need a new bumper as I doubt if the existing one can be straightened out.'

Now in fact this driver could have a very good case, but his letter presents it in the worst possible way. He has waited two days before writing to the insurance company but he still appears almost incoherent with annoyance. He should have restrained his annoyance but written without delay along lines such as the following:

```
Dear Sirs,
    I was driving east in the right-hand
lane along the Brompton Road at 2.30 p.m.
on Sunday, May 4th at about 25 miles an
hour. Traffic was slight. The weather was
clear but the roads were slippery from a
recent heavy shower of rain. On passing
the main entrance to Harrods I noticed,
some 30 yards ahead of me and moving
slowly in the same direction in the
left-hand lane, a yellow Cortina (Reg.
No. .....). The Cortina was moving at
little more than walking pace but
suddenly, and without any warning, made a
sharp right turn, apparently as part of a
U-turn. On reaching the right-hand,
east-ward bound lane, the driver was
prevented from continuing his U-turn by
traffic moving in the west-bound lanes.
I braked as hard as was possible, and, on
approaching the Cortina, pulled hard down
on my right-hand lock so that I hit the
vehicle at an angle rather than head-on.
The damage to the Cortina appeared to
consist of no more than a couple of dents
in the off-side door panel but the wing
of my car (Reg. No. ....., covered by
your Policy No. .....) was badly damaged,
```

```
the headlamp wrecked and the bumper so
damaged that it will probably require
replacement.
   The driver, who gave his name and
address as ..... and his Insurance
Company as the ....., asked why I had not
seen him. I replied that I had seen him
but that he had given no warning
whatsoever of his move. He made no reply.
A Mrs ..... of ..... who stopped after
seeing the impact says that she saw the
Cortina start its U-turn but does not
recollect seeing any warning sign.
U-turns are forbidden on this stretch of
road, but I am not certain whether the ban
includes Sundays.
                          Yours faithfully,
```

Many kinds of insurance claim can involve writing to solicitors but this is not necessarily difficult or complicated and in most cases, whether dealing with insurance or not, you will initially be asking only for an interview. Having made your request, all that is needed is to set down a very brief indication of the matter you wish to discuss. It will, in fact, usually be sufficient to say no more than:

```
Dear Sir,
   I am seeking advice concerning a clause
in the will of my father who died abroad
some weeks ago and would be grateful for
an appointment with you in the not too
distant future.
                          Yours faithfully,
```

The bank

Much the same formula applies to most letters to your bank. In general, it is best to be brief, although you could, if you felt it might be helpful, add a short note of explanation.

```
Dear Sir,
    I would be glad of a short discussion
about certain of my financial affairs and
will telephone your secretary within the
next few days to see when would be
convenient.
    I wish to add a small extension to the
house at the above address which I own
freehold. The estimated cost is about
£1000 and I would like your advice on the
best way of financing this.
                        Yours faithfully,
```

The information will allow the Bank Manager not only to study your statements for the last few years, which he would probably do anyway in the circumstances, but to consider them in the specific light of the matter you have raised. With such exceptions, however, it is better to leave details to be discussed face-to-face with him.

It may sound strange to link the bank with letters of complaint. However, bank staff are no more infallible than other mortals and it is not unknown for two sorts of mistakes to be made, one of which occurs when the bank sends you someone else's statement, with or without your own. In this case return the wrong statement immediately. A note of surprise, saying that this does not increase your confidence in the bank, is fully justified; but of course do not say anything which would suggest that you had looked at the wrong statement in detail.

In addition, errors in bank statements are not unknown. They should be brought to notice without delay – but without rancour. Thus:

```
Dear Sir,
    I notice that on page 23 of my statement
which I received today, a sum of £53 has
been credited to my account apparently in
error. As you will see from your records
I have paid in no such sum during the
period covered and have no such sum
```

```
outstanding to me. I would be grateful for
your comments and for the correction that
appears to be necessary.
                         Yours truly,
```

Apologies

It is to be hoped that you will have checked your statement very carefully before making a complaint. However, computerised statements give less information than those we used to receive and it is always possible to go wrong when checking up. If it is you, rather than the Bank, that has made a mistake, you can of course just let the matter rest; but there is very rarely any harm in admitting that you have been wrong, so a short note along these lines would not be out of place·

```
Dear Mr Smith,
  Thank you for your letter of the 14th
May. I now realise what the position is,
and see that the mistake was mine and not
yours. I hope you will accept my
apologies.
                         Yours sincerely,
```

A letter of apology can be called for if you have forgotten to do something that you promised to do, so there is a brief but useful routine that should be gone through before you put any letter in the post. Read it through once more and see if there are any matters in it about which you should make a note.

If, for instance, you have promised to put something in the post unless you hear from your correspondent within a week, put a reminder of this in your diary several days ahead. And if you have said 'I will give you a telephone call within the next few days', then jot down a note to make that call.

If in spite of your good intentions you have not put that something in the post, or have not made the promised telephone call, the best way out of the difficulty is to be honest. Circumstances will alter cases, but the following opening would be suitable for most letters of apology:

```
Dear Mr White,
   I am writing to you in some
embarrassment and with many apologies.
You will remember that in my letter to you
earlier this month, asking. for advice
about buying some furniture, I said that I
would telephone you within a few days.
You must be wondering why I have not done
so.
```

At this point, what you say will very much depend on the truth. It is hardly reasonable to say 'I just forgot' and far better to apologise by explaining the reasons behind such forgetfulness. The sort of sentence to use is:

```
Unfortunately, I was unexpectedly called
away on business, and in the complicated
rush that followed failed to do as I had
promised.
```

The reverse of an apology is called for if you have received a letter obviously intended for someone else but put into an envelope addressed to you. Here something as brief as possible is required, such as:

```
Dear Mr Green,
   I have just received the enclosed letter
which has been addressed to me in error,
so I am returning it herewith.
                              Yours truly,
```

You should not, of course, say that you have, or have not, read the whole letter, which might cause additional embarrassment. Obviously you will have read some of it since the envelope was addressed to you, but you will probably not have got very far before realising that it was not for you; so it is better to say as little as possible.

Incidentally, one way of yourself avoiding such embarrassing errors, which are most likely to occur when you are writing half a dozen letters in succession, is to write each letter, address the envelope, and then seal up the letter before going on to the next one.

5 Business Letters

In his classic book of advice on how to write good English, *The Complete Plain Words*, the late Sir Ernest Gowers quoted from an Inland Revenue Staff Instruction. Its injunctions should be remembered by everyone writing any kind of letter, but in particular by those dealing with business correspondence. 'There is one golden rule to bear in mind always', the instruction says, 'that we should try to put ourselves in the position of our correspondent, to imagine his feelings as he writes his letters, and to gauge his reaction as he receives ours. If we put ourselves in the other man's shoes we shall speedily detect how unconvincing our letters can seem, or how much we may be taking for granted.' That is true whether you are writing for a job, resigning from one, complaining of non-payment or trying to sell goods to a potential customer.

Job applications

Of all the letters that you are ever likely to write under the heading of 'business', one of the most important will almost certainly be that in which you are applying for a job. A good letter certainly does not guarantee that you will get the post for which you are applying; on the other hand, a poor letter goes a long way towards ensuring failure, however good your actual qualifications may be. Therefore give a great deal of thought to what you want to say before you actually put pen to paper or paper to typewriter.

As a rule you will usually describe your background as far as it is relevant to the job, and here the first question is not so much: 'what shall I put in?' as 'what shall I leave out?'. To start at the beginning, it is as well to make some reference to your educational background. How much of this you give will depend not only on your accomplishments but on how far back they were achieved. If you are in your late teens it is quite relevant to list your school record, your O-levels or A-levels and the subjects in which they were gained. However, if you are in your late twenties or more it may seem strange to a prospective employer that you make so much of what you achieved a decade or more back. He is probably far more interested in what you have done during the past few years. If, then, you are in this category you could say merely: 'I was educated at St Botolph's Comprehensive School, where I took 3 A-levels' (without mentioning the subjects unless they would be particularly relevant). However, any university degrees, diplomas or any technical or professional qualifications should be mentioned, even if they are not directly relevant to the job for which you are applying.

Achievements which have a direct relation to the job should of course be stated, although a word of warning is needed here. If you are a very young man applying for a post with a firm which manufactures sporting equipment it will be useful if you can mention that when at school you captained your cricket Eleven. If, however, you are in your thirties, it would be advisable to consider whether your prospective employer might not regard this as a sign of backward thinking. It would probably be best left to the interview.

If you are applying for your first job, your letter is comparatively easy in one respect since you do not have to describe your present work. If you are already employed, however, it is essential that you give an adequate account of what you are doing. 'At present I work for one of the directors of Williams & Sons' is not very informative. More useful would be a sentence which said: 'For the last three years I have been employed by Williams & Sons, have worked for the director who has special responsibility for exports, and am therefore accustomed to writing to customers in Europe and the United States.' And here, of course, you would refer to your proficiency in any foreign languages. Be honest, however, and remember that 'Fluent French' or 'a good working knowledge of French' are very different from stumbling tortuously through French correspondence. It would also be useful if you could say, for instance: 'I have a good working knowledge of French, written and spoken. As regards the latter, I spent three months, two years ago, living with a family in Rouen.'

In listing your personal qualifications there are good and bad ways of doing this. A bad letter would run like this: 'When I went to Paterson and Company four years ago I was merely a junior assistant to the Research Director. He discovered, however, that I was particularly good at handling other workers and within eighteen months I was put in charge of a section with a dozen workers in it. Since then I have been promoted to control of a second section and now have two dozen men working for me.'

To take the last point first, the workers are not, in fact, working for you but working for the company. Also, while you may have stated the facts accurately, your letter betrays a bombast which might well make an employer think: 'I wonder if he'll cause trouble with my staff.' But you could give the same information, and create a much better impression, if you said something like this: 'I joined Paterson and Company four years ago as an assistant to the Research Director, was subsequently put in charge of a small section in the laboratory and am now in charge of two sections in which a total of twenty-four men are employed.'

A potential employer who has read the details of what you are doing at present will then naturally ask himself: 'Why is he leaving?' There may be a perfectly reasonable answer to this, and if so you should put it down, accurately but briefly, early in your letter. You might, for instance, be able to say: 'I am answering your advertisement as Paterson & Company, for whom I am working at present, are moving their works to the north of England and I do not wish to leave London.' If you can supplement this by an additional explanation such as '... because I do not wish to disrupt my children's education', that will help to banish the idea that you are a stick-in-the-mud with a dislike for what an increasing number of firms consider essential mobility. Or there might be another reason such as: 'There is little chance of Paterson & Company expanding in the near future and I am looking for a fresh appointment in view of the lack of promotion prospects.'

Another possibility is that you have got the sack, or been made redundant as it is now usually called. In times of depression and contracting trade, being made redundant does not carry the stigma that it would in other circumstances. There is no point in hiding the fact in your letter of application. It will almost certainly come to light if you are successful in gaining an interview. It is unlikely to count as a black mark against you if you can say something like: 'I have been made redundant after six years at Patersons due to the contraction of their business and their consequent decision to close one of their works.' What you should not do in any circumstances is to suggest that you have a grievance, even if you are justified. You do not say: 'Even after six years unbroken work for Paterson and Company they have now made me redundant.' Put that way, your prospective employer may well wonder not only why you were picked for redundancy rather than someone else, but may write you off as a grouser.

If there are, in fact, reasons for being made redundant that you do not wish brought to the notice of a new employer, your best chance of success lies in diplomatically stressing the advantages of the new job as you see them. You might, therefore, be able to say: 'My present salary is roughly the same as you are offering, but I am attracted by the area in which you operate and by your very pleasant working conditions.'

You should, of course, be careful about such phrases, as you should not write anything which could be construed as damaging to your current employer. It is not the possibility of libel that matters here – except in very unusual circumstances – but that no one is likely to take on a new employee who complains about his current employer. Whatever their qualifications, workers with chips on the shoulder are rarely wanted. Incidentally, if the advertisement gives only a Box Number, you would be advised to look for the phrase 'present staff notified': it could have been issued by your present employer. However, if you have put in your application no more than the truth and have not grossly exaggerated the importance of the work you are doing, it is unlikely that any harm will have been done – except, of course, that your present employer will know that you are looking around elsewhere.

When you have made a draft of your letter of application, look at the advertisement carefully once again, and make certain that you have complied with all its requirements. If references are asked for, make sure that you have them, and if five copies are required, send five and not four. If age, current earnings and full *curriculum vitae* are asked for, make sure that you are including them. The first candidates likely to be eliminated are those who do not conform to the requirements of the advertisement.

There is one exception to this last injunction. You may feel confident that you could satisfactorily fill a post which you see advertised even though you lack one of the qualifications. It may be that you are a year or two over, or under, the age limits laid down, or that you have served only eight instead of ten years, as asked for, at a certain level. It is always possible that the advertiser will receive no one with *all* the qualifications he requires; it is even possible that he did not expect to, but asked for so much in order to attract as high a standard of applicant as possible. You may well feel you have a chance, so go ahead; but you should make it clear that you have read the advertisement properly but believe that you have a special case to put forward. In these circumstances you could end your letter with a brief paragraph such as this: 'In view of my long experience in handling this type of account, and of my very varied experience in so many sectors of the computer industry, I have felt justified in answering your advertisement even though I am slightly outside the age limits which you lay down.'

Finally, there is the all-important overall effect created by your letter. Try to put yourself in the position of the man who will read it. Does it suggest that the writer is hardly confident of himself; or does it suggest that he is so over-confident that something must be wrong? Is there a phrase which suggests too much self-esteem, or another which suggests too much modesty? This is a matter which only you can decide, however much advice you may seek from friends. However, if you have been completely honest you are unlikely to have gone far wrong.

References

Employers nearly always ask for references, if not in their initial advertisement at least at a later stage, and it is as well to have three or four names ready. The people whom you involve in references will depend to some extent on the sort of information they are expected to give about you. Many employers want information on character rather than qualifications, and local clergymen have for long been popular for this reason. Even today, when the links between church and laymen are steadily diminishing, there will be many situations in which a clergyman is better qualified to provide a reference than anyone else, although a local businessman or local Councillor who has known you for some while would of course be satisfactory. But, whether or not you feel that the local clergyman is the best person to provide a reference, you should always, before giving the name of any referee, make certain that he has no objection to your giving it. He could be approached by a letter like this:

Dear Mr Tawney,
    Now that I have completed my course at the Rodney Technical College I shall be applying for my first job, and I would be most grateful for your help on one matter. I think it very likely that I shall be asked to give the name of one or two persons who have known me for a number of years and to whom application could be made for a character-reference. If I could have permission to give your name I should very much appreciate it, since you have known our family fairly well since you came to the district almost a dozen years ago.
                                        Yours sincerely,

In giving character-references, the rules to be followed are really the same as those which have already been noted in the case of private references. Thus if you, rather than the local vicar, were asked to provide a reference for a youth who had been to the same school as your son, you could answer in one of two ways:

```
Dear Sir,
     Thank you for your letter asking for a
character-reference for --. I have known
him for the last ten years and as he
has been a fairly constant companion of
my son have had good opportunity for
seeing him under varied conditions. He has
always seemed to me to be a youth of
admirable character, straightforward and
honest, and always anxious to put his
shoulder to the wheel. I myself would be
glad to employ him if my business had any
suitable opening for him.
                         Yours truly,
```

Alternatively, you might feel that something like the following was needed:

```
Dear Sir,
     Thank you for asking for a character-
reference for --. It is true that I have
known him for ten years and that he has,
for much of that period, been a companion
to my son John. But I am afraid that I
have not really had a close enough
acquaintance with him to be of use to you.
                         Yours truly,
```

One can assume that in the case of the second letter you will not have been forewarned. But what if you *had* been asked by the youth, and wanted to refuse for what you felt was a proper reason? In that case you could have replied to him along the following lines:

```
Dear Joe,
   Thank you for suggesting that you
should give my name as a character-
reference when applying for a job. I
would certainly like to help you, but in
this case there is a difficulty which I
think you will appreciate. John has known
you for a number of years and you have
visited us here more than once. But a
reference of the kind you would be looking
for should come from someone who has
known you far more closely than I have,
and anything I could honestly say would
not therefore be very helpful. I believe
that if you think carefully you will be
able to produce the names of those who
will be of far more use to you than I
can be.
                    With the best of wishes,
                           Yours sincerely,
```

Following the letter of application for a job there comes – one hopes – the letter of acceptance. Your employer may well send you a formal letter but if he does not do so you should confirm the appointment in a letter such as this:

```
Dear Sir,
   Thank you for appointing me your deputy
clerk at a salary of £— a week. I
understand that my duties will commence
on June 1st and I look forward to taking
them up on that date.
                           Yours faithfully,
```

Letters of resignation

At first sight, it would appear that the task of writing a letter of resignation should offer no difficulties at all. This is far from true. Even if you have already got another job and therefore have no need of a reference now, an employer whom you have

served for some time could always be the source of one in the
future. There is therefore every good reason for parting on good
terms whatever your personal feelings may be, although something will depend on whether your employer knows, or suspects,
that you have been looking for another job. But a little courtesy –
and even of 'flannel' – will do no harm. So a tactful letter could
go something like this:

```
Dear Mr Wilkinson,
    As I think you know, I have for some
while been anxious to move to a company
where my interest in exports would be
given greater scope. In the nature of
things it is unlikely that the
Wilkinson Company's expansion will be in
this direction, and I have now secured a
post as export manager of the Guildhome
Company. While I wish to join Guildhome
as soon as possible I am most anxious to
cause the Wilkinson Company, with whom I
have had good relations over the last six
years, as little inconvenience as
possible. Our formal agreement stipulates
a month's notice on either side but I
would be willing to stay on until the rush
of the present season's order is over –
that is for the next six weeks – if this
would be helpful. If you could let me
know about this within the near future I
would be most grateful as the Guildhome
Company is naturally anxious to know at
what date I shall be free to join them.
                        Yours truly,
```

If you are the person receiving the letter of resignation, it can,
in much the same way, be counter-productive to appear churlish.
Whatever your private feelings, it would be stupid to acknowledge a resignation along the lines of: 'I am surprised that after
the long service you have given to this firm you have decided to
leave us.' Good employers are not surprised and, in any case, if a

man has given long service he should be thanked for it. So why
not:

> Dear Mr Mackie,
>   I am sorry to hear that you are leaving
> us after having given us such good service
> for so many years. Nevertheless, you have
> my best wishes in what I hope will be a
> happy and profitable new job.
>   Yours sincerely,

Reprimands

While it is the employee who has to use care when he starts
writing a letter of resignation, it is the employer who has to
exercise his judgment in the matter of issuing reprimands. And
the word 'employer' in this context does not necessarily mean the
head of a company employing hundreds of men. Even if you have
only a handful of staff, many of them perhaps working for you
only half-time, you may nevertheless find it necessary on occasion to write this sort of letter. When you do so you will in at
least one way be in much the same position as the managing
director of a multi-national company ticking off one of his departmental managers: you will have to ensure not only that your
letter is written without bias or prejudice, but that no bias or
prejudice even appears to be present in it. 'Justice must not only
be done but must be seen to be done.'

To start with, are you reprimanding the right person? If there
is any failure on the part of a subordinate, a reprimand should
normally be addressed to his superior, for three very good
reasons. It is the task of the superior to ensure that those under
him perform their duties properly and if you tackle the offender
direct, you are going over the head of the superior officer and
thereby creating bad feeling. Secondly, a superior may be
directly responsible – if, for instance, he has sent a porter on an
errand which has taken the porter away from his post. Finally,
the superior may know of extenuating circumstances.

But, assuming that no superior is concerned, first ask yourself
a few questions. Do the facts as you know them inevitably lead

to the conclusions you have drawn? The fact that a letter never arrived is not proof that it was never posted. An unanswered telephone does not, necessarily, mean that there was no one manning it, since a faulty line can result in the caller hearing a ringing tone even though the subscriber's bell is not ringing. Are you relying only on hearsay evidence, which in most cases is decidedly unwise? How serious is the offence for which you feel that a reprimand should be issued? In other words, are you 'making the punishment fit the crime', or are you preparing to write a letter that will remain on the files when a personal word to the man concerned is really all that is needed? And are there any extenuating circumstances, such as illness, domestic anxiety, pressure of work, or the fact that an employee was, possibly against his own wishes, standing in for someone else?

All these questions may seem unnecessary. Nevertheless, it should be remembered that a written reprimand will probably be filed and thus go 'on the record'; will probably stay there for years; and if made hastily or unfairly can sour relations that might otherwise have improved. So reprimands should never be written in haste and should in all but a few exceptional circumstances admit that there may possibly be an explanation of the lapse involved. Here is the right and the wrong way. At first glance the differences may seem small, but they are nevertheless important.

A bad letter would go like this. 'I have today heard from Messrs. Smith and Co. that you have not replied to the letter which they sent us a week ago. I have told them that such a dereliction of duty on the part of any member of our staff is most unusual and I have informed them that I will be reprimanding the person concerned. Will you please answer Messrs. Smith and Co. without delay and see that this lapse is not repeated.'

A safer – and fairer – way of writing would be:

```
Dear Jones,
    Messrs. Smith and Co. told me today that
they had not yet received a reply to the
letter which they wrote to you a week ago.
I have assured them that delay in
```

answering correspondence on the part of
any member of our firm is most unusual,
and have told them that I am asking you to
find out what has happened.
    If either their letter or a reply from
you has gone astray in the post would you
please get in touch with them at once. If
it has been received, please reply to it
without delay, offering your apologies and
at the same time let me know what
happened.

Yours truly,

The first letter claimed that Messrs. Smith and Co. were saying that no reply had been written, whereas they would almost certainly have said that no reply had been received. The statement regarding 'dereliction of duty' would be very unwise unless it could be capable of proof in a court of law, while the statement regarding a reprimand and the use of the word 'lapse' might well be considered unjustified.

Dismissals

Reprimands are in general as free of Government interference as resignations. The same is by no means true of dismissals and the employer who wishes to sack an employee, and the employee who receives his notice, will both be aware that they are circumscribed by a host of rules and regulations. In the following suggestions, therefore, it must be taken for granted that the writer knows these rules and regulations – which are constantly changing – and is not trying to evade them in any way. What is being discussed, is thus not so much the fact of dismissal as the problem of the way in which it can best be presented. It is one which has to be solved not so much by big companies – where a good deal of impersonality inevitably governs affairs – as by the hundreds of small businessmen and shopkeepers who have to sack men, or women, whom they may have known personally for years.

At one end of the scale there is the letter which just says brutally:

Dear Mr Black,
 I am hereby giving you the necessary
four weeks notice of termination of
engagement, to expire on May 1, after
which date your services will no longer be
required.
                              Yours truly,

At the other end there is the letter which starts:

Dear Mr Black,
 It is my most unpleasant duty to tell
you that I am no longer able to employ you
and must ask you to accept formal notice
from today's date. This step, which I and
my colleagues on the board are taking most
reluctantly, has been forced on us by the
contraction of business. We are all
appreciative of what you have done for us
and I hope that we shall be able to show
this when we come to discuss the terms of
your severance pay and the date on which
you will actually be leaving us. I shall
be glad to supply references and to aid in
any other way possible in helping you to
secure another post. But we can of course
talk about this when we come to financial
matters. Perhaps you would telephone my
secretary to fix a time when we can meet.
                              Yours truly,

In practice letters of dismissal normally come somewhere between these two extremes but there is one point that should always be borne in mind. Whatever the circumstances, you should never write anything in a letter of dismissal that could in any way be construed as defamatory. Quite apart from dishonesty, which only the most naïve would mention in a letter, there are other things which should not be hinted at. Carelessness, inability to get on with other members of the staff, bad time-keeping, and various other failings which you might well be able to substantiate, should nevertheless be omitted.

Transfers

While a letter of dismissal is one of the most difficult that an employer has to write, an employee can find that there is one situation which is quite as tricky from his point of view. Until the last few years, the typical specimen of this species would have been a request for transfer to another branch of the bank, insurance company or firm for which you work. Today, with firms far more mobile, the typical letter is more likely to be a request that a transfer should *not* be made. As circumstances so often alter cases, here the relevant factors are how much you have been t old officially, your company's reputation for good or not-so-good treatment of their employees, and your own personal chances of employment if you refuse to be transferred But a letter written on the following lines will suggest the way to proceed.

```
Dear Mr James,
    I understand (or, if suitable), I see from
the news in the latest issue of the staff
bulletin (or even), judging by reports in the
local papers (but remember that they may be
wrong) — that the finishing department is
to be moved within the next twelve months
to Newnham-on-Sea, but that some members
of the department will be found work in
the existing factory. I should like to
make the strongest possible plea that I
should be one of those members. You will
see from the records that I have worked in
the present factory for twelve years, but
this alone is not the main reason for my
wish to remain here. I am mid-way through
buying my own house and while I know that
the company is generous both in helping to
find accommodation and in providing money
```

for removal expenses, neither my wife nor
myself really wish to move to a new
district so far away. The situation is
further complicated by the fact that both
of us have elderly relatives nearby.
  I am certain you will appreciate that
the situation is causing us considerable
anxiety and I would be most grateful to
know, as soon as is reasonably possible,
the position regarding my future
employment with the company.
                        Yours sincerely,

It may – or may not – then be expedient for you to add a
following paragraph which would say: 'Although I have always
enjoyed working for the company I am afraid I would find it
very difficult to remain an employee if this involved moving
our home.' You might, of course, write 'impossible' instead of
'very difficult' but this would be distinctly unwise since it is
almost the equivalent of offering to sack yourself.

If this is the first occasion on which the company has been
considering a move, you would be justified in asking a number of
pertinent questions, particularly if you had not made up your
mind against the move as definitely as suggested in the above
letter. In this case you could say after your opening sentence:
'I myself am not anxious to move and would prefer to be
numbered among those members of the department remaining
in the present works. However, I would be grateful if you could
tell me what help will be given to transferred workers in finding new accommodation and in paying for their removal expenses.'

Sales letters

'Sales letters' is a phrase that covers everything from the car
salesman's offer of a secondhand Rolls-Royce to the duplicated
letter pushed through the letterbox and seeking custom for
plumbing or painting services. Nevertheless, all sales letters
have a great many things in common.

The ideal first rule, but one which it is often impossible to follow, is that a sales letter should be addressed only to someone who is a potential customer. It is a waste of time and money to advertise dog food to someone who has no intention of owning a dog or to solicit support for a car cleaning service among people who do not own a car. In more general terms there would be little point in circularising the occupiers of lower-income flats with details of Bond Street-type jewellery; and just as little in circularising those in luxury flats with details of cut-price do-it-yourself services.

A certain amount of 'wastage' is usually inevitable in any large-scale distribution of sales letters. Names and addresses are often taken from reference books or the membership lists of professional bodies and while this is useful in some fields – in selling new legal books to lawyers for instance, or flowers and seeds to members of the local horticultural society – the method should be used with care. Even where specialised lists are used, the method is not always plain sailing. The growing spread of launderettes, for instance, appears to have hit 'old-fashioned' laundries and at least one, trying to maintain turn-over, decided to inaugurate a high-class laundering service for men's shirts which it described as 'shirt services'. It was certainly reasonable to advertise this among existing clients. However, *all* of them were circularised, and although the letter was well-written, the percentage response was less than had been expected. One reason, no doubt, was that the addressees included a number of single women who had never sent a male garment to the laundry in their lives. Most will have realised that they had become involved in local mass-advertising, but when they considered the laundry's claim to give each customer personal service, the letter became counter-productive.

The example illustrates the second rule about a good sales letter. Make absolutely sure that it does not contain anything which might reasonably annoy the person receiving it. With some obvious exceptions, the writer of a sales letter is unlikely to know to what political party his potential customer will belong. It is, therefore, most unwise to make any statement which can even indirectly be construed as having political overtones. In addition, avoid if possible any reference to religious or racial groups. Finally, as a case of 'great-care-required' if not of 'avoid altogether', there is humour. Nothing is worse than a joke that falls flat, and unless you are exceptionally good or exceptionally lucky, a joke that is included in a sales letter is likely to infuriate quite as many people as it amuses.

Once you have appreciated the possible pitfalls, the things to be avoided, it is time to turn to the positive aspects of the sales letter. Here the first point to be made is that a sales letter which is anything less than completely honest deserves to fail and very often will fail. This applies both to the use of physical description and to wider claims as well. 'In mint condition', 'scarcely used', and 'almost new' are phrases which should be used only if they will stand up to close scrutiny. But it is also inadvisable to say, for instance: 'I sell the world's best and cheapest', while the word 'guarantee' should only be used with care. It would be unwise to say: 'I guarantee that you will never regret buying from us', but it might be permissible for you to write: 'I can guarantee that I have been the owner of the car since it was first registered.' In the same way, you should write: 'I provide a 24-hour service', only if you do always provide that – not if you only provide it sometimes.

Many businesses have potential customers in very different social groups and it is often difficult to decide whether one selling letter is suitable for all of them or whether it is better to have more than one letter available. This is not a matter of 'class' in the old and increasingly outdated sense. It is rather an admission of the fact that different people have different requirements. To illustrate the point one might consider a small printer whose business is mid-way between a new block of luxury flats and another block which has obviously been erected for lower- and middle-income families. Both blocks will contain a number of potential customers, but the letters that go to them should be subtly different.

Most residents of the first block will probably believe that private notepaper should be die-stamped rather than printed, and the following would be a good selling letter to address to them.

```
Dear Occupier,
    You may be interested to know that we
are able to offer a 48-hour die-stamping
and printing service for the convenience
of customers who have recently moved to a
new address or who for some other reason
require fresh supplies of headed
notepaper at short notice.
    We can offer an excellent choice of
stationery as well as a wide variety of
sample headings, and can guarantee a high
standard of workmanship. As you will see
from the enclosed price list, our charges
are extremely reasonable.
    We would draw your attention to
postcards printed with name, address and
telephone number at ... per 1000 and to
the fact that if you have any quantity of
unused writing paper bearing a former
address, it may be possible to guillotine
this before die-stamping or printing with

your new address.
    Our order department is open from 8.30
a.m. until 6.00 p.m. on weekdays,
including Saturday, which is frequently
convenient for busy people who find it
difficult to call in normal business
hours.
                            Yours faithfully,
```

The recipients of this letter do not have to be sold the idea of using headed notepaper, but will probably appreciate good value for money, good service and business enterprise. Occupants of the second block may well feel that printed notepaper is a luxury and the first task will therefore be to sell them the idea of even considering it. One possible opening would be as follows:

```
Dear Occupier,
    You are no doubt glad to show your new
home to those of your friends and
relatives who live near enough to visit
it, but what about those who live too far
```

away? A letter on your own headed
notepaper is an easy way of telling them
where you now live and at the same time of
making quite certain that they do not
misread the new address, which can happen
more easily and more often than we
sometimes imagine. Moreover the cost is by
no means high as you will see from the
price-list that we enclose.

Yours faithfully,

Alternatively, there are the very practical advantages of
using your own notepaper which could be stressed like this:

Dear Occupier,
   When you want to write to someone rather
special, you may hunt for a sheet of
paper and envelope, and may sometimes have
to put off writing until the next time the
shops are open.
   Writing pads can get lost or dirty or
even used up for scribbling, but printed
notepaper complete with matching
envelopes, and safe in its box, is a very
different matter. Paper and envelopes
always look clean and attractive, and that
itself takes away a little of the
drudgery that sometimes goes with
letter-writing.
   Whether you are applying for a job,
asking for a rise, or just dropping a line
to friends you met on holiday, headed
notepaper creates a good impression right
from the start.
   Having your own stationery was once
thought of as an extravagance. Nowadays
the situation is very different, as you
will see from our enclosed list of
charges. In fact a trial box of 100 sheets
and 50 envelopes will cost you only ......
which is very little compared with some of
the items in most weekly budgets.

Yours faithfully,

It is not only in the context of such direct sales that a good letter can make so much difference. And it is not only 'business-men' in the narrow sense of the word who are concerned. Thousands of men and women throughout the country who run boarding houses or only let rooms – quite apart from those who run small hotels – can benefit by using tact and imagination in their replies to potential clients.

A typical example would be that of a boarding-house keeper in one of Britain's popular mountain areas. A holiday-maker asking if accommodation was vacant, and enquiring what the cost would be, could well add the following sentence: 'My wife and I are interested in mountain-climbing and also in the possibilities of doing some simple scrambling. Could you tell me if there are any mountain guides in your area?'

Now the person who receives this letter may have come to the area only recently, and may have no special wish to attract ramblers and scramblers. He or she might therefore be tempted to deal with the queries about accommodation and terms, and then add: 'I am afraid that I do not have any information about mountaineering instruction.' This in itself is hardly encouraging. Ignorance of what will probably be at least a minor local 'industry' suggests that the writer may well be equally unable to help with such things as the local bus timetables. A few local enquiries would enable the following far more helpful reply to be sent:

```
Regarding your enquiry about
mountaineering instruction, I am sorry to
say that there is none available in the
village. However, there is a bus service
to the head of the valley and regular
daily courses are held there by the ......
Group (address) ..... who will no doubt be
able to help you. In addition, there are
four fully qualified guides living not too
far away and I understand that all have
proved very satisfactory to previous
visitors to the area. Their names (given
in alphabetical order since I am told that
all are equally competent) are as
follows .....
```

These are comparatively simple examples of how best to sell your goods and services. It should always be remembered, however, that certain precautions should be borne in mind when writing letters offering goods or services, or which accept them. We are not concerned here with cases of dishonesty, or of a firm taking deliberate advantage of customers. That sort of thing is increasingly covered by the law. Far more important are the genuine misunderstandings which can arise if one or both sides fail to say plainly exactly what it is that each is selling or buying, together with the conditions of sale.

The most obvious of such conditions can be date of delivery. A confectioner might, for instance, be ordering four hundred Easter eggs. But he would be well advised to write into his order the stipulation that they must be delivered by, for instance, mid-February or whatever the date by which he thinks they will be needed. Otherwise, he might have difficulty in refusing to pay for them even if they arrived only a few days before Easter.

In much buying and selling no formal contract is exchanged, and in such cases it is the final written acceptance of an offer which in effect becomes the contract. This means that acceptance should contain the delivery date and anything else which is relevant, including any matters that have been agreed only verbally. It is always possible that the full details of the transaction have been outlined in previous correspondence and if so it is permissible to simplify matters by saying, for instance, that the contract is subject to the conditions which you have set down in your letter of a specific date. But make this precise and refer to one letter which you know has been acknowledged; i.e. '. . . as outlined in my letter to you of January 23rd.'

You may wonder why it is necessary to put down in writing details which you have agreed with someone whom you know you can trust. The point at issue is not one of honesty but of commonsense. If some disagreement arises in the future the man with whom you deal could be dead, or could have left the firm with whom you are dealing. You are therefore quite justified in taking precautions in business matters which in private correspondence would suggest you were abnormally suspicious. Even if you are conducting business with a friend or a relative there is no reason for being less than businesslike. If you sense that you are appearing too suspicious you can always point out that you wish all your contracts, agreements, etc. to be found correct down to the smallest detail should there be an emergency.

More business disagreements arise through honest muddle and misunderstanding than through dishonesty, and it is essential to keep the chances of muddle to a minimum. One all too frequent cause of misunderstanding is failure to make it clear whether a letter in reply to an offer is an acceptance or merely a show of interest. Suppose, for instance, that an office equipment firm, knowing that you are interested in certain items, has sent you a letter saying:

```
Dear Sir,
   In connection with your recent enquiry
we can offer you a good re-built electric
Adler Model ..... £150; a good re-built
Adler Model ..... £100; and a new but
shop-soiled Lumoprint duplicator,
Model ..... at £105.
                        Yours faithfully,
```

If, after considering the offer, you feel that you are merely a potential buyer, you could reply as follows:

```
Dear Sir,
   Thank you for the offer of the three
items of office equipment detailed in your
letter of December 1st. I am certainly
interested, but before ordering any of
these would wish to try them out in our
Broad Street office. Would it be possible
for you to let me have any, or all of
them, for a one- or two-day trial?
                        Yours truly,
```

Or, if you feel that the prices are high, you could well say so and ask: 'If all three were bought together would it be possible for you to offer a discount?' Either letter, or any letter couched in such terms, will make it clear that you are not ordering the equipment.

If, however, you have decided that you do want to purchase, there will be little point in replying: 'Thank you for your offer of the three items of equipment listed in your letter of December 1st. It seems that they will meet our requirements very well, and the price seems to be about right. I would be grateful if you could let me know about delivery.'

The receiver of such a letter could very well assume that you had ordered the three items. However, you do not say so in so many words, while the final sentence suggests that your acceptance might be conditional on delivery being by a specific date. In these circumstances you might very well find that the goods had been sold to someone else.

This would be avoided if you replied like this.

```
Dear Sir,
    Thank you for your letter of December
4th offering us a good re-built electric
Adler Model ..... at £150, a good re-built
Adler Model ..... at £100 and a new but
shop-soiled Lumoprint duplicator, Model
..... at £105. We accept your offer and
would be glad if you would deliver the
three machines as soon as possible. In
view of certain commitments we must make
our acceptance conditional on the machines
being delivered within four weeks, but I
imagine that there is no problem about
this.
                         Yours faithfully,
```

You will note that you have not only listed the three items but have repeated the firm's 'good' and 'new but shop-soiled'. There can, of course, always be argument about how good is 'good' but you will, however, have given yourself some protection if any of the machines turns out to be unsatisfactory. You will, in any case, almost certainly be protected to some extent by recent consumer legislation although there are, of course, two self-protecting steps which you should take as a matter of course:

inspect the equipment personally before entering into any negotiations and deal only with a firm which is well-established and has a reputation for fair dealing.

As we have already noted, most troubles arise in business from genuine misunderstanding and this is particularly true when the matter involves not a physical object, such as a piece of office equipment, but a mixture of service and accommodation. All too often small businessmen get caught up in embarrassing circumstances that could have been avoided by giving a little additional thought to the letters written. Typical of many was that of a one-man firm whose proprietor was building up a successful business in hand-made jewellery. He heard that the Chamber of Commerce in a large nearby town was preparing to hold an Industry Fair and thought that it might be useful if he took a stand and exhibited his wares. All he needed to say in writing to the organiser was something like this:

```
Dear Sir,
    I would be grateful if you would send me
details of the Industry Fair which you are
organising in Extown later this year,
including the costs of hiring a display
stand.
                              Yours faithfully,
```

Instead, what he wrote was this: 'I have heard that you are organising an Industry Fair in Extown later this year. I think that it would be a good place for me to display examples of the hand-made jewellery which is made in my workshop here, and I would like to do this. Please send particulars – I hope it is not too late to book a stand, as I know that this sometimes has to be arranged a very long time in advance.' This was a bad letter on many counts but above all because it failed to put across one important fact: that the letter-writer was merely a potential exhibitor and wanted to know how much a site in the Fair would cost. It is true that his letter might not be taken in a court of law as a contract to take space, even though many hoteliers receive letters just as unbusinesslike from clients who expect a room to be reserved for them on the strength of nothing more definite.

However, the jewellery-maker was shocked to receive a letter which said:

```
Dear Sir,
    Thank you for your letter of January 4.
As you thought, space begins to book up
more than a year ahead and all the space
had been booked when I received your
letter. However, this morning's post
brought a cancellation and I have
therefore reserved for you one of our
standard display areas, six foot by eight
feet at the standard rate of five pounds
per square foot. The fee of two hundred
and forty pounds (£240) is payable at once
and I shall be glad to receive your
cheque together with any further
instructions regarding decoration of
stalls which can be carried out in
accordance with the enclosed schedule of
charges.
                        Yours faithfully,
```

The only places where the craftsman had previously exhibited his jewellery had been at small village events and he had not expected space at the Industry Fair to cost more than £20–25. But he now compounded his mistake by doing nothing until he had a reminder about the £240 in a letter which said that the date for cancellation was past. He then wrote the following: 'I am sorry that I have not replied earlier to your first letter. I was honestly surprised to get your letter this morning since when I wrote I was really only making a general enquiry about taking space. I did not realise that the charges would be as high as they are, and it would never be worth my while to display my goods like this. I do hope that you will therefore agree to my cancelling my order as a small business like mine could never stand the expense.'

This was a poor letter in its phrasing and a worse one in that it specifically spoke of 'cancelling' an 'order'. The organiser of the Fair had been doing his job as a salesman and trying to turn a potential buyer into a real one but until the use of the word 'order' he would have had very little chance of making an issue out of it.

In the circumstances the jeweller should have responded to the first letter in terms such as these.

```
Dear Sir,
    Thank you for sending me particulars of
the Industry Fair for which I asked in my
letter of January 4. I have, however,
decided against taking space at this
event.
                            Yours truly,
```

Alternatively he could, as a precaution, have gone to his solicitor who could have sent a letter to the organiser discouraging him from making any formal attempt to secure payment in such a poor case. The letter to the solicitor, which should have been accompanied by a carbon of the original letter to the organiser and a copy of the reply, should have gone like this.

```
Dear Mr Black,
    I recently enquired about taking space
at the Industry Fair to be held later this
year and have received a reply from the
Organiser who has erroneously taken my
letter as an order. I am enclosing a
carbon of my letter and a copy of his. I
would be grateful if you would write to
him pointing out that I have placed no
order. I will telephone you about this
within the next two days.
                            Yours sincerely,
```

The point about telephoning is that if the solicitor has any minor points that he wishes to raise they can probably be settled more quickly – and more cheaply – by a few words on the telephone than by an exchange of letters.

Overdue payments, orders etc.

Retrieving yourself from a situation in which you have made a mistake is only one of a number which calls for a careful mixture of tact and firmness. The same is true when you are demanding money in settlement of an unpaid account. The position will to some extent be governed by your own judgement on whether lack of payment is due to an oversight, an attempt to avoid payment, or an inability to pay. You are unlikely to be sure of the answer and it will usually be wise to send a first letter along the following lines.

```
Dear Sirs,
   We note that our account for £314.40,
dated May 4th, 19—, has not yet been
settled. As you know, our conditions of
sale include payment one month from
invoicing, and I imagine that the delay
has occurred owing to the present busy
state of the trade. Nevertheless, it is
now seven weeks since date·of invoicing
and we would much appreciate settlement.
                     Yours faithfully,
```

If this fails to produce payment within a week a sterner note is called for:

```
Dear Sirs,
   We have still not received settlement of
our account for £314.40 dated May 4th,
19—, and must now ask for settlement
without further delay.
                     Yours truly,
```

Only if no payment follows swiftly would it be suitable to take the next step, that of sending a letter along the following lines:

```
Dear Sirs,
   Having received no acknowledgement of
our letters of June 24 and July 1, and no
settlement of our account for £314.40
dated May 4th, 19—, we shall reluctantly
```

```
be forced to put the matter in the hands
of our solicitors if payment is not made
by return.
                              Yours truly,
```

The same policy of 'hurrying slowly' is usually the best to adopt when writing business letters of complaint, whether the trouble is bad workmanship or non-delivery. In the case of the latter it is always wise to realise that the fault may not lie with the supplier. He may, in fact, be just as perturbed as the non-receiver who will gain little from adopting the 'unless' attitude. It is bad policy, for instance, to write: 'Only six of the dozen photographic enlargers ordered last May have so far arrived. We are now running up to the post-holiday period when we have our biggest demand, and unless the missing six arrive within the next fortnight I shall refuse to accept them.' Before putting your complaint on paper it is essential to look at your order and at the supplier's note of acceptance. You may then find that you cannot, in any case, 'refuse to accept'; alternatively, you may find that you can refuse. But in neither case would the above letter be a good one. If there is nothing in the order stipulating date of delivery, the following letter would be suitable.

```
Dear Sir,
    Six of the dozen photographic enlargers
which we ordered from you last May have
not yet been delivered. I am certain you
will appreciate that the post-holiday
months which will soon be with us are by
far the best for sales of enlargers. We
are hoping to encourage these in this area
and trust you will do everything possible
to ensure that we do not run out of stock
at the most favourable time of the year.
                              Yours truly,
```

Even if there is a stipulation in your order that the goods must arrive by a certain time, an unnecessary cancellation will do little to ensure adequate service in the future. In these circumstances it would be suitable to write as follows:

Dear Sir,
  We have still not received six of the
photographic enlargers ordered from you
last May. As you will see from the order
the final date for delivery is only a week
away. Your firm is no doubt as anxious as
we are to ensure that this equipment is
put on the market this month when some of
the holidays are already over and
circumstances are so good for sales. Can
you, therefore, please let us know without
delay whether we are to receive the
enlargers by the stipulated date?
                       Yours truly,

The answer to this last letter might, if you were unlucky, be
along the following lines:

Dear Sirs,
  Thank you for your letter of .....
dealing with delivery of enlargers. I am
sorry to say that the makers have been
having labour problems, and it seems
likely that we shall only be getting some
three-quarters of our promised supplies.
As wholesalers we are as anxious to
supply the goods as you are to sell them,
but will understand your position if you
feel it necessary to cancel the order for
the outstanding items. May we suggest that
you wait until the end of the month and
that we review the situation then.
Meanwhile, we will put all possible
pressure on the manufacturers.
                     Yours faithfully,

In such a situation you might feel it necessary to hold a
meeting with your sales staff and, afterwards, to write a brief
account on what had taken place. The need for a concise record,
less formal than a fully-blown report but nevertheless describing
a meeting in some detail, is by no means confined to those in

'big business'. Even if your firm is only a small one it will be useful to have on record an objective account of what happened when matters affecting the firm's future were discussed. If you are writing a report to a partner or to a superior it can form part of the body of the letter, but it is usually better to write it out on a separate sheet and refer to it in the letter.

Reporting meetings

To take an example rather more important than the one just dealt with, consider the case where there had been discussion about the site of new premises. You would, if it were your job to report on the meeting, refer to it briefly in the accompanying letter which would say: 'John Brown came to discuss the site of the new premises and I am enclosing an account of the meeting we had with him.'

The account should be strictly objective. In other words you should not allow your own opinions to become mixed up with what Mr Brown reported – although you can of course put your views at the end of the report if you felt that they were called for. You should also remember that the account may be passed on to others who do not have as much background as you have, and you should therefore make your report self-contained and should include all the relevant information. And, above all, avoid woolly statements. First, the sort of thing to avoid: 'Mr Brown came to discuss his views on where the new premises should be sited, and although he brought his labour expert with him I was not much impressed by what he had to say. His accountant whom he also brought along with him may be right about that Government support we might obtain, but I really think that other factors, which I pointed out in our discussion, are far more important and I really don't think we should go into Linkthorpe, even though most of the other possibilities were ruled out.'

Instead, head the sheet of paper with something like this:

```
Report of a meeting held in the offices of
Camdex Ltd., Burnt Road, Cheswall, on
```

March 9th, 19—, to discuss the best site
for the proposed new assembly works.

> Present: John Brown, chief technical
> consultant, Brown and Cranford,
> architects.
> James Wright, chief accountant,
> Brown and Cranford.
> Anthony Pringle, labour
> manager, Brown and Cranford.
> Ronald Tucker, Deputy Chairman,
> Camdex Ltd. (the present
> writer).

After this, the report could continue as follows:

Mr Brown said that as instructed he had
made a survey of possible sites for the
new assembly works within ten miles of the
main factory. Two – those at Crumbley and
Overstall – had been quickly ruled out,
since it was discovered that the
freeholders were not prepared to lease on
realistic terms, or to sell. A possible
site at Hambleford, which was in many
ways ideal, has poor communications and
although, as Mr Brown pointed out, it
would be possible for us to provide works
buses for the comparatively small number
of staff who would be involved, he felt
that the isolation of the area had
already given it such a reputation that we
might find it difficult to attract
workers. Mr Pringle felt even more
strongly that this would be the case. Two
sites at Maggotsford and Brandon were
ruled out when Mr Brown reported that
local building restrictions would almost
certainly prevent us from erecting the
works to the specification most
convenient for us.
Mr Brown then went on to say that he had

investigated the sixth site, at
Linkthorpe, and considered that this was
the best available. Mr Pringle
commented that while labour was scarce in
this area, he thought that Camdex had a
good enough reputation to attract the
comparatively small numbers that would be
required. Mr Wright supported Mr Brown on
the grounds that Linkthorpe lies just
within one of the local development areas;
and thought it possible that at least
some Government support might be
obtained.

My own view is that the Linkthorpe site
would, in practice, have disadvantages as
great as that at Hambleford. Labour of the
right quality has been a problem on
previous occasions and I suggest that
before going ahead with Linkthorpe we
should make another effort to find a more
suitable site. Before this is done, the
possibility of going slightly farther
afield might be investigated. Perhaps
Mr Durley, our transport manager, could
give us a brief note on increased costs,
etc. if the new assembly works was
twelve or fifteen miles away.

6 Selling Abroad

In the nature of things, very many letters written to foreign countries will be business letters, and special care will naturally have to be taken with them. Letters to holiday friends you have met on the Continent should present no particular problems and the same is obviously true of correspondence with in-laws or other relatives who are not of your own nationality. Business letters are a totally different matter, and here you have first to take a decision on one important point. Should you write in English or in the language of the man or woman you are writing to?

There are some foreign countries in which letters written in English are accepted as perfectly normal. India, for instance, which has a large number of local languages and dialects, and an inheritance of British rule over centuries, finds letters in English acceptable; the same is true of many Middle Eastern states. In the Scandinavian countries a letter in English will almost always be understood, although one written in the recipient's own language is likely to give the writer a little advantage over competitors who omit this courtesy. Elsewhere, however, and certainly in most of the Common Market countries, as well as in others in Europe, a letter in the language of the man you are writing to is the usual thing.

If you are fluent in the language of your correspondent, all well and good, for you have no problem. Unfortunately, however, not everyone is a good linguist, and for those who are not there are two alternatives. The first is to draft your letter in English and have it translated and typed. Most towns of any size have efficient translation agencies, and while their fees may at first sight seem high the money is invariably well spent. The alternative is of course to write in English; this is clearly a second-best but there are some circumstances in which it can be inevitable. The one thing to avoid, at all costs, is to attempt to use a language in which you are not perfectly at home in the truly colloquial sense. It is only too easy to cause offence unwittingly; in addition, the wrong use of a word or phrase can all too readily lead to business misunderstandings, and even to legal difficulties if you have intended to say one thing and have in fact said something slightly different. Anyway it is good policy to get your letter competently translated. Ignorance never inspires confidence.

Before you actually start writing to a foreign client it is to be hoped that you will have made yourself familiar with some of the ways in which his background life is different from your own. Although none of the following may enter directly into your early correspondence it can later be useful if you know that the public holidays are different from those of England; that business hours on the Continent tend to start earlier and end later, but include a two-hour lunch break during which all business ceases – a break that in Spain, for instance, can be as long as three-and-a-half hours; and that the structure of local Government can – as in France with its pyramid of department, arrondissement, canton and commune – be more complicated than in Britain. And do not forget that there is very often a time difference between Britain and the countries on the other side of the Channel.

Remember, also, that every Continental country has its own conventions regarding modes of address which are almost without exception more formal than they would be in Britain. Thus in France 'Monsieur' is used even before 'President' which means both Chairman and President. Europeans tend to be rather more particular than we are in Britain about formalities, and a little trouble taken in getting things right will usually pay dividends. Here it may be as well to stress what may seem the blindingly obvious – that every Embassy worth its salt has an official whose task it is to straighten out the more obvious problems that the small businessman has to face. Many countries have separate import–export or trading groups, and the fullest use should be made of them, particularly before negotiations are opened for the first time with a foreign country.

Every country – even England, Ireland, Scotland and Wales – has its own traditions and its own conventions as to the way that business is done. Accepting these is not kow-towing but merely the sort of courtesy which oils the wheels of trade. Here again, guidance from the Embassy, or from its trade counsellor or his equivalent, is the obvious thing to seek if you are not fully acquainted with conditions in the country you are writing to.

The Middle East

While the need to brief yourself properly on conditions abroad, to 'do your homework' as it were, is necessary when dealing with European countries, it is even more important when writing to the Middle East. Here convention, climate – and, not least, religion – are all so very different from those in Britain and Europe that it is easy to put a foot wrong without realising it.

Conventions are at last beginning to change, very largely under the impact of links with America, but there can be important differences between Middle Eastern countries which lie next to one another on the map and which, it could be assumed, would have customs in common.

However, this is the general advice given by an expert with long experience of trading in this area:

1. Remember that any sign of brusqueness can be interpreted as lack of interest. A sense of proportion is obviously called for; there is no need to lard a letter with flowery terms, but what might sound rather extravagant in a letter to a British firm could be just right in one going to the Middle East.
2. Unless you know your correspondent very well indeed, avoid personal enquiries or expressions of interest in his family affairs.
3. When you receive a letter from a Middle East correspon-

dent, make certain that your reply is sent off as quickly as possible. Businessmen in this area prefer to carry out their business by means of personal contact rather than by correspondence, and a letter to Britain therefore tends to show enthusiasm. Maintain this enthusiasm by sending a prompt reply. Here it is as well to warn that even if you have successfully started negotiations with a Middle East client, he will almost certainly expect you to follow them up with a personal visit.

Setting-up Abroad

There are naturally exceptions to any rule, but it is as well to remember the words of the expert: 'Letter-writing is not, in general, relied on as an adequate means of communication with customers in the Middle East who usually prefer to deal with people on a personal basis.'

Even the comparatively small businessman may have contacts with foreign countries that involve more than buying and selling. He may, for instance, wish to set up in business abroad, having first checked, of course, that there are no impediments as far as any British regulations are concerned. In this case it is absolutely essential to gather as much information as possible before making any plans. The first step would be to write a brief letter to the commercial attaché's department in London. It could go along these lines:

```
Dear Sir,
    I am anxious to set up a small assembly
works near the town of ..... and would be
grateful if you would let me know to whom
I should send particulars of my proposals.
                         Yours faithfully,
```

The answer will of course depend on the country. The likelihood is that you will be advised to write first to a department of the country's central government, although in some cases you may be referred to a regional authority. In either case, you should ask a number of pertinent questions. Your letter could go like this:

Dear Sir,

I am contemplating an extension of my business as manufacturer of specialised do-it-yourself equipment into ...... The Trade Counsellor at your London Embassy has suggested that I should get in touch with you and I shall be very grateful for any help which you can give me.

The firm of ..... was founded by me at the above London address in 1955 and our turn-over has steadily built up to its present figure of £..... per annum. Many items in our range are in great demand in your country and I have for some while been considering setting up a small factory for their assembly, employing between forty and fifty local people in the ..... area.

I would therefore much appreciate it if you could let me have details of the present position on the following matters:

1. What permission is required from local or other authorities for the setting-up of such a factory?

2. What is the current availability of labour in this area and what are the regulations governing its employment? In Britain some 75% of our semi-skilled workforce consists of women and I am wondering whether a similar proportion of local women workers would be acceptable.

3. While about 50% of our materials could be bought locally, we would wish to import a number of components (listed on a separate enclosed sheet) for assembly in the new factory, at least until provision was made for their manufacture locally rather than in Britain, and I would like to know

what, if any, import duties would be
levied in these circumstances.
4. I would wish to employ three or four
British foremen, at least for the
first year of the factory's operation
and would be glad to know whether
work permits would be granted to
them.
5. Are there at present in force any
specific laws which you feel might
affect the successful running of such
an assembly works?
I shall, of course, be glad to visit you
to discuss the matter in detail at any
mutually convenient time.
                                    Yours faithfully,

While correspondence with Europeans tends to be slightly
more formal than letters between Britons, the reverse is the case
when dealing with the United States, or, for that matter, with
Canada. Therefore one might think that it is easier to write a
successful business letter to North America than to France or
Germany or Italy. But this doesn't by any means follow.

North America

One of the biggest illusions is that the British, Americans and
Canadians all speak the same language! But it is not only the
catch-phrases and the boss-words that are different. There is a
freer – and some people would say less grammatical – approach
to writing that can easily make some English letters sound stilted
and somewhat formal. Two small but significant differences
show up when one considers the start and the ending of a letter.
In the United States, the progress from 'Dear Sir' to 'Dear Mr
Jones' to 'Dear Jim' is accomplished far more quickly than in
Britain. In fact it is increasingly rare to find the 'Dear Sir'
approach used at all. Even though you have never met your
correspondent it will be almost taken for granted that when you
write to him for the first time you will begin: 'Dear Mr James'.

So, too, with the ending of a letter. 'Instead of 'Yours sincerely', 'Sincerely' is normal even in the early stages of a correspondence while 'Yours cordially', which might look affected in a letter to an Englishman, could seem natural enough to an American. And remember that 'Esquire' is not used in North America. So you write to 'Mr Cyrus Matson', never to 'Cyrus Matson, Esq.'.

Quite apart from this difference in the formalities, there are differences in the language itself. Some words mean one thing in Britain and something else in North America and that something may even be the reverse of the British meaning. A case of the former is the word billion. In Britain this means one million million (1 000 000 000 000, frequently written 1 000 000M) while in the United States it means one thousand million (1 000 000 000 or 1000M). As an example of a word meaning one thing in Britain and its reverse in the United States, there is the verb 'to table'. In Britain, 'tabling' a motion means that it is set down for discussion; in the United States it means that the motion is set aside rather than discussed.

In addition to the words and phrases that are likely to crop up in business correspondence there are others that can easily cause confusion. Thus in Britain a 'public school' is of course a fee-paying – in fact a non-public – school, whereas in the United States the phrase has the more straightforward meaning of a school used by the public, in other words roughly a local authority primary or secondary school. What the British call a bill is a 'check' in the United States, a 'blue point' in the United States is a particular sort of oyster and in Britain a particular sort of cat, while what British sportsmen call a 'gun dog' is known as a 'bird dog' on the far side of the Atlantic.

Now it is obviously impossible for a writer who has never been to the United States, let alone lived there, to be aware of all these pitfalls – but there are in existence one or two good and relatively cheap English–American 'dictionaries' and anyone likely to be writing to the United States regularly would be well advised to invest in one of them. Failing this, however, try if possible to show a draft of your opening correspondence with America to someone who is likely to spot any obvious errors.

Another point which should be remembered when writing to

anyone in the United States is not merely the size of the country but the differences in outlook between one part and another. The flourishing, and more conservative, cities of the Eastern seaboard are not only as far from California as London is from Beirut but their outlooks are almost as different. Remember that the United States has no 'national' daily newspapers in the British sense of the phrase. East coast and West coast are separated not only by the Rocky Mountains but the thousands of miles of rolling prairies making up the Middle West. So if you are doing business with someone in San Francisco the fact that you have already been successful in Boston will not necessarily help very much and may even be a handicap since local conditions can be so very different.

So first, how not to go about it. Consider this letter to Mr Cyrus Rockefeller, President of a large printing agency in San Francisco.

```
Dear Sir,
     As the manufacturers of a unique form of
photographic printing equipment which has
been successfully on sale throughout the
Continent of Europe for more than
twenty years, we are anxious to sell our
products in North America and would like
to know whether you would consider
handling this equipment.
     Our firm has been in existence since
1820, and our products are of a solid
reliance which has brought them tributes
from satisfied users in a dozen
Continental countries.
     I enclose a printed prospectus giving
details of the equipment and would be glad
to have this demonstrated to you should
you be visiting the United Kingdom. I
myself may be visiting the United States
later this year and would be glad to
discuss details with you in New York.
     I have the honour to remain,
               Sir,
                    Yours very truly,
```

To start at the beginning, the 'Dear Sir' should be 'Dear Mr Rockefeller' or even 'Dear President'. Next, 'unique' is a very dangerous word to use unless you are completely up-to-date with the latest developments in the United States. In addition, the fact that your equipment has been successfully in use for more than twenty years could easily produce the reaction: 'What, twenty years old! Surely there must be something better by now.' Then the phrase 'North America'. This includes Canada as well as the United States, another country with different laws, traditions and, in many ways, requirements. The fact that your firm has been in existence for more than a century and a half is not necessarily a recommendation, while the phrase 'solid reliance' can well suggest to an American something very different from what it means to you. Instead of 'dependable and never breaking down', the picture summoned up to an American could well be 'old-fashioned and cumbersome'. The suggestion in the last paragraph that your potential customer should go out of his way on your account would be bad enough in any letter and here it is compounded by the idea that he might be willing to make a transcontinental trip of some 2500 miles just to see you. Finally, the 'honour to remain, Sir' and the 'Yours very truly' might convince your correspondent that Britain was still living in the age of Charles Dickens.

The following would have a far greater chance of success:

```
Dear Mr Rockefeller,
    The latest model of our photographic
printing equipment with its quick
production of immaculate results is
particularly suited to the demands of a
richly-developing State such as
California. We have been searching for a
forward-looking group which would be able
to handle its sale and believe that yours
might be the ideal Corporation to do this.
    I enclose with this letter our latest
brochure giving details of what this
remarkable equipment will do and a list of
the terms on which we have successfully
extended its use in other countries.
```

Although we are about to market the
latest models in other countries, we have
not as yet approached the United States.
I shall, of course, be delighted to
arrange a demonstration for you in San
Francisco so that you can assess the
value of the equipment for yourself.

If there are any further details which
you would like to have, I will ensure that
you receive these without delay.

Sincerely,

In other words, be friendly, offer service, and have no inhibitions about praising your own goods. That advice should be
followed in virtually every business letter you are ever likely to
write to a correspondent in the United States.

7 Miscellaneous

So far we have been dealing with letters written for purely personal or business reasons. However there are other kinds of correspondence, including postcards, invitations and even form-filling, which require that you put pen to paper.

Letters to newspapers

There still remains the letter to the newspaper, almost a British hobby and written for a variety of reasons. You may wish to make public a complaint or ventilate some grievance against the authorities; you may wish to ask for information; you may wish to air your opinions – which other people can of course always call your prejudices! – on some matter in which you are a specialist; or you may wish to state your views on a subject of public importance which is being nationally debated. Whatever your reason for writing to the editor, two points should be remembered.

The first is that every newspaper in the country receives, every week, many many times the number of letters which it is able to print. With the best will in the world, those chosen are a selection of a selection, and there is no real justification for feeling disgruntled if yours is not among them. The second point is that virtually all editors reserve the right to shorten letters before they are printed. Without the existence of this proviso they would face a difficult task and would be able to carry it out only by printing even fewer letters than they print at present. When shortening letters a newspaper should, of course, alter neither its sense nor its balance. Whether or not this is done can easily be the matter of controversy; and while the majority of papers deal fairly with their correspondents it is easy for a writer who has carefully balanced up half a dozen points to feel that the balance has been altered. If this happens, the most sensible thing is first to ask the opinion of someone who is not personally involved – with you, with the paper, or with the argument. If the verdict, after a reading of what you wrote and what was printed, is that a distortion has been made, a further letter may put things right. Thus:

```
Dear Sir,
   In printing my letter on divorce on
May 24 I notice that you omitted the
fourth paragraph. I appreciate that some
shortening of letters is often necessary,
and that in this case the point left out
may at first sight appear to be a minor
one. However, in the opinion of those who
have studied the subject deeply the
qualification I made is in fact of
considerable importance and I would be
grateful if you would make it clear that
after dealing with the question of
custody I wrote  ............'
                           Yours truly,
```

You may not be lucky. But if you fail with this kind of letter you are pretty certain to fail with any other kind. You can, of course, complain to the Press Council, but you would be advised to do this only if the incident has involved an obvious and flagrant distortion.

How do you start with a letter to the Editor? In many cases you should start by blowing your own trumpet. If you wish to add to the debate about the training of mountaineers it will obviously help if you can start: 'As a member of two Everest expeditions, and with experience of Alpine climbing during a dozen seasons. . . .' In a different field, it would be useful if you could begin: 'As a member of the most recent Commission which considered the possibilities of a Severn Barrage, I have naturally followed the argument about power from Britain's rivers in your recent correspondence columns.' Keep a sense of proportion, of course. If you start your letter by saying: 'As a member of the Little Morton Lawn Tennis Club I feel qualified to offer some advice about the current Wimbledon controversy', it may be better for your reputation if your letter is not printed.

Next, you should recapitulate at least briefly what the controversy is about. You may have followed the argument blow by blow, but not every reader of the paper will have done this. So, for instance, after your opening comment about having been a member of the Severn Barrage Commission, you might go on:

```
Some of your readers, notably Mr Smith in
his letter of May 4, have claimed that a
series of barrages could solve our energy
problems completely. Others, such as Mr
Jones in his letter of May 9, maintain
that the money spent on such schemes will
be entirely wasted. As I will try to show
by the following figures, neither of these
correspondents are really justified in
their statements.
```

You should remember that even in correspondence with relatively small local papers, your letter is likely to be scrutinised by a number of genuine experts, while if it is printed in a national newspaper you may have some of the best brains in the country trying to pick holes in it. This is no reason for timidity, or for failing to write, but it is a reason for going over your letter when it has been written and checking every detail you have put down. If you are wrong on even a very minor point you will have opened the way for any opponents to cast doubt on more than this small error – 'I notice that Mr James fails to give even the correct date on which the first contribution to the controversy was made, and I am therefore wondering what reliance can be put on any of his more complicated and more important figures.' So take extra precautions to get even the smallest fact quite correct.

Another point to watch if your letter deals, for instance, with complaints about local affairs, is the use of dangerous overgeneralisations. After talks with your neighbours, you may be tempted to start a letter with the words: 'Everyone in Larkspur Street agrees that the proposed construction of new licensed premises at the bottom of the street is most unwelcome and will, if carried out, lower both the tone of the street and the value of the houses in it.' Now it is extremely unlikely that such a statement would be true; and even if it were you would probably have some difficulty in substantiating the fact. 'Everyone' means everyone. What you really mean is that a number of friends and acquaintances agree with you. There is no escape from the word 'everyone' and if you use it you may encourage a letter saying, for instance: 'Mr Smith is completely wrong in claiming that everyone in Larkspur Street objects to the proposed new licensed premises. I for one regard it as an additional amenity and believe that there are many other residents who think as I do. I hope that if any protest is being planned – which I personally would much regret – it will at least be organised on sensible grounds and not make itself look ridiculous by the exaggerated claims which often make protest movements look more ludicrous than rational.' In such a case, the one enthusiastic word 'everyone' would have done the cause little good.

Letters to the newspapers are often used to arouse interest in the commemoration of local people or local events. In such cases, the choice usually has to be made between a letter so long that it will probably be drastically cut or one which fails to provide enough detail. It is sometimes possible to avoid this difficulty by first writing to the editor a letter which is not intended for publication. It could go something like this.

```
Dear Sir,
     As you no doubt know, next year marks
the centenary of the birth in Hamchester
of the architect Sir James Gilmore who not
only designed many of the most important
buildings in the town but who has
achieved some fame for his other works
throughout the country. I and a number of
interested friends are anxious to
commemorate Sir James's birth, possibly
```

```
by a public exhibition in the town, or in
some other suitable way, and I am
wondering whether you would be willing to
give publicity to such proposals. I would
be glad to outline what we have in mind,
and would be grateful to know the length
of any letter dealing with this to which
you would be able to give space.
                        Yours faithfully,
```

Such a letter might very well produce a call from one of the paper's reporters and this would enable you to outline your plans in detail. At the very worst you might get a reply saying that, due to pressure on space, your letter should be kept down to two hundred words or so. If you have considered spreading yourself over a couple of columns the editor's suggestion may sound like squeezing a gallon into a pint pot. However, all that you really have to say at this stage is something as follows:

```
Next year will see the centenary of the
birth in Hamchester of the well-known
architect, Sir James Gilmore who died in
1957. I am hoping to organise an
exhibition to commemorate the event and
would be glad if anyone who might be able
to help would get in touch with me at the
above address.
```

In a case like this you would presumably write similar letters to the specialist journals of the architectural press. You would probably know what they were but if not – the Public Library again! – you would find details of them in one of the various Press directories.

In any letter to the Press you will, of course, take particular care about libel. It is true that all newspapers are very well aware of the danger and that many of them permanently employ a lawyer who reads proofs of the pages in an effort to ensure that nothing libellous is actually printed. Nevertheless, the number of libel cases which reach the courts – only a percentage of those which are settled out of court – is an indication that lawyers are not infallible.

There is one special point to be watched here. You might, for instance, write in all honesty: 'There is really no reason why the views about the safety of the new electric grid expressed in your issue of June 4 by James Todd should be taken more seriously than those of anyone else.' The newspaper might have no reason to suspect that there was anything dangerous here. But if Mr Todd was in fact a senior electrical consultant the position would be rather different; and if he could show that an important item of professional work had not gone his way because of the effects of your letter, your situation could be difficult.

As a final point, be prepared for even a single short letter in a local paper involving you in lengthy correspondence that can go on for weeks. You have been warned!

So far we have been dealing solely with letters, the pieces of paper which you put into an envelope which is then sealed and stamped and posted. There are, however, other ways of writing which have their own advantages – as well as disadvantages.

Postcards and letter-cards

First of all, certainly in popularity, there is the postcard, which today comes in a variety of versions which would have astonished our grandparents. The simple postcard, quick and easy though it is, nevertheless has certain disadvantages of which the most obvious is lack of privacy since anyone who picks it up can read it. But the postcard has always been useful for such simple messages as: 'See you on Tuesday at 6.30.' Only the message should be written on a postcard, there being no 'Dear .....' and no 'Yours sincerely' at the end. But the date should go in the top right-hand corner. One point to note is that the message should not run over on to the side of the card where you write the name and address of the person to whom you are sending it.

In addition to the plain, non-picture, utility card, there is of course the huge range of 'holiday' postcards, ranging from the 'fat lady on the beach' variety to those showing local views or local monuments. These are all of the 'wish you were here' variety and the rules to be observed in using them are the same as those for ordinary cards – no 'dear's or 'sincerely's.

The cards that go into envelopes were until fairly recently limited to Christmas and New Year cards, together with a small range of those sending congratulations on births, birthdays and marriages. Today the range is almost limitless and it is possible to buy printed cards which welcome a householder into his new home, wish him the best of luck on a journey, welcome him back home, or congratulate him on passing an examination or his driving test, quite apart from those which just say 'get well quickly'. These cards really need little more than a signature to which an additional single-line message can be added. However, many people – and not all of them middle-aged or elderly – regard the sending of such cards as a rather second-best and perfunctory way of dealing with an occasion. A handwritten note, however brief, shows a good deal more personal feeling.

In addition to postcards, there are the letter-cards which can be bought at Post Offices. They are of particular use to people who are travelling, have no stationery with them, and want to send something more private than a postcard. With a letter-card, you write what you want on it, then fold it over and seal it so that its contents cannot be read until it is opened. Similar in appearance to letter-cards are Air-Letters, forms printed on especially light-weight paper which can be used and sealed in much the same way.

There are also invitation cards, sometimes printed, sometimes with only portions printed with the gaps to be filled in by the sender. Such a card will carry an invitation in the third person, see illustration on p. 144.

An invitation should always be answered in the same person as that in which it is sent, so that in this case the reply if the invitation is accepted, should be: 'Mr and Mrs Frank Jones thank Mrs James Smith for her kind invitation to an At Home on September 13 and have much pleasure in accepting.' One point to note here is that those invited 'have' much pleasure in accepting, not 'will have', the explanation being that while the At Home is to be held in the future, the invitation is being accepted now. The same is true if the invitation has to be refused: 'Mr and Mrs Frank Jones thank Mrs James Smith for her kind invitation to an At Home on September 13, but much regret that due to a

---

Mr. and Mrs. Frank Jones

Mrs. James Smith
at Home
on Tuesday, September 13th.

R.S.V.P
43 Truslove Street   *6-8p.m.*
London W.3

---

prior engagement they are unable to attend' – 'are unable' and
not 'will be unable'.

Filling in forms

While more letters are probably being written now than were
being written in the past, the number of forms which have to be
filled in is also increasing. And, surprisingly enough perhaps,
there are quite a number of mistakes in form-filling that can be
avoided by a little thought. Although the forms that the average
man or woman has to fill up include those for a television
licence, a driving licence, a car licence, a children's allowance,
and perhaps for the despatch of a packet abroad, there are
certain commonsense rules to be observed with all of them. The
first is to read the form carefully from beginning to end before
you begin to fill it in. And when you start to do that, remember
that most forms must be, and all forms should be, completed

either in pen or on a typewriter, except for the signature which must be handwritten. Pencil is not good enough. Start at the beginning and with your pen work your way through to the end, remembering that there are probably places or boxes where you have to put a tick or a cross. Many forms also include alternative phrases or even alternative sentences which except for the appropriate ones have to be scored through. These may vary from: 'I am/am not over 21' to 'Please credit the proceeds to my account No. .... at ..... Branch of .... Bank/ Please send me a cheque for the proceeds.' If you fail to do the necessary crossing-out, back will come the form. There are other cases – notably the forms which have to be filled in for Value Added Tax – where if the answer is 'None', the word 'None' must be written in, a simple dash being insufficient.

Overall, the most important thing with form-filling is to take the greatest pains to be absolutely accurate in the answers that you make to any questions. Failure to give the correct answer can, for instance, invalidate an insurance policy or lead to considerable trouble if money is involved in the payment of pensions or allowances.

Since telephoning has taken the place of so much letter-writing it is appropriate to mention a few points about the use of the telephone that almost certainly seem self-evident but are in fact often ignored. With the cost as high as it is, the first thing to suggest is that you do not telephone at 5.45 p.m. if the cheap rate comes into operation at 6.00 p.m. The second thing, if you are ringing a business firm, is to make clear who it is you want to speak to. 'A Mr Jones who has something to do with buying' will probably take a lot more time (and money – yours) to find than: 'Mr Henry Jones in the buying section of the export department.' And of course if you can give an extension number for him so much the better. An alternative, which can be useful if you are dealing with a very big organisation, or if you are not certain whether the person you wish to speak to will be there, is to make a personal call. Although there is an extra charge made by the Post Office for this, the normal charge only starts when you begin speaking to the man or woman you want, while if he or she cannot be found there is no charge at all. Having got your connection, state who you are and what you want to discuss – and remember to have a pencil and pad always handy by the telephone.

8 Methods of Address

When the final draft of a letter has been completed, three more matters must be decided.

1. Mode of address – that is, the opening words of the letter, e.g. 'Dear Sir'.
2. The conclusion – that is, the formal ending which immediately precedes your signature, e.g. 'Yours faithfully'.
3. The superscription – that is, the form in which the name of your correspondent will appear on the envelope, e.g. 'The Right Honourable Sir John Smith, PC, DSO, MP'.

In each case there are some rules so definite that even the most progressive would regard their infringement as a sign of discourtesy, ignorance or slovenliness. There are others on which some latitude is permissible so that, within limits, the writer may use his own discretion. In doing this he should take into account the known (or reasonably presumed) views of his correspondent, the degree of acquaintance, and the relative status of the person addressed and of himself.

In case of doubt it is better to err on the side of formality, though not to the extent of being archaic or ridiculous. The mode of address and the conclusion must 'match'. A letter beginning 'Dear Jones' should end 'Yours sincerely' or 'With kind regards' not 'Yours faithfully'.

The most formal mode of address to those without titles is simply the single word 'Sir' or 'Madam', written on a line to itself and in the same place as the more usual 'Dear Sir'. There was a time when this was the polite form of address when writing to any official or any stranger. Nowadays its use is much more restricted, the un-prefixed 'Sir' or 'Madam' being used only as a sign of great respect to someone of importance, such as the Sovereign, or the Sovereign's immediate relatives or personal representative, such as a Governor-General, or the Prime Minister. In an ordinary letter this form of address would be so formal as to suggest hostility or at least a chilly politeness.

A doctor, of any faculty and of either sex, who has no other title is normally addressed simply as 'Dear Dr Smith' unless he (or she) is either a surgeon or a doctor of medicine who has attained consultant status, in which cases the correct form of address is 'Mr, Mrs or Miss Smith'.

A professor (even if also a Doctor) is addressed as 'Dear Professor Smith'.

If the doctor or professor has any other title (peerage, baronet-age, knighthood, Service or ecclesiastical rank, or one derived from a high appointment, such as a judgeship) this technically takes precedence, so far as addressing him at the beginning of the letter is concerned.

When Dr Smith becomes a Canon he should be addressed as 'Canon Smith'; when Professor John Smith becomes a knight, he should be addressed as 'Dear Sir John'. If Canon Smith inherits a peerage title, or Sir John has one conferred upon him, then both become 'Dear Lord Smith'.

While this is the correct procedure, there are one or two holders of multiple titles who prefer to be known by that which they value most rather than that which technically ranks higher. A man may set more store by his professorship (which he earned for himself) than by his baronet's title (which he may have inherited). If you know this to be the case it is courteous to respect his personal preference.

Non-commissioned officers and commissioned officers of the lowest ranks (that is, up to and including sub-lieutenants in the Royal Navy, lieutenants in the Army and pilot officers in the RAF) are addressed by their civilian ranks whatever these may be, as 'Dear Mr Smith, Dear Dr Smith, Dear Sir John, Dear Lord Smith,' or 'Dear Miss (or Mrs) Smith'.

Above this level the service rank takes precedence at least as long as the holder is a serving officer. Captain Sir John Smith should be addressed as 'Dear Captain Smith' and Admiral the Earl of Eyton as 'Dear Admiral Eyton'. These are the correct forms and should always be used when writing to officers on matters connected with their service duties, e.g. when writing to the officer commanding a local unit.

Ranks in the Royal Navy, Army, and Royal Air Force

ROYAL NAVY	ARMY	ROYAL AIR FORCE
Admiral of the Fleet	Field-Marshal (FM)	Marshal of the RAF
Admiral	General (Gen)	Air Chief Marshal
Vice-Admiral (Vice-Adm)	Lieutenant-General (Lt-Gen)	Air Marshal
Rear-Admiral (Rear-Adm)	Major-General (Maj-Gen)	Air Vice-Marshal
Commodore (1st and 2nd Class) (Cdre)	Brigadier (Brig)	Air Commodore (Air Cdre)
Captain (Capt)	Colonel (Col)	Group Captain (Gp Capt)
Commander (Cdr)	Lieutenant-Colonel (Lt-Col)	Wing Commander (Wing Cdr)
Lieutenant-Commander (Lt-Cdr)	Major (Maj)	Squadron Leader (Sqn Ldr)
Lieutenant (Lt)	Captain (Capt)	Flight-Lieutenant (Flt-Lt)
Sub-Lieutenant (Lt)	Lieutenant (Lt)	Flying Officer (FO)
Acting Sub-Lieutenant	Second Lieutenant (2nd Lt)	Pilot Officer (PO)

Commissioned ranks in the Women's Royal Army Corps and the Women's Royal Air Force are the same as those in the Army and the Royal Air Force. In the Woman's Royal Naval Service, the equivalents are as follows:

ROYAL NAVY	WOMAN'S ROYAL NAVAL SERVICE
Commodore	Commandant
Commander	Chief Officer
Lieutenant-Commander	First Officer
Lieutenant	Second Officer
Sub-Lieutenant	Third Officer

This rule originated in the days when the Armed Forces consisted almost entirely of regulars who would normally remain on the active list throughout their professional careers. The advent of the 'civilian army' and the short-term commission have made some latitude desirable on the grounds of commonsense.

If Lord Smith saw only war-time service with an emergency commission, and has been demobilised for the past thirty years, it is unlikely that he would wish to be addressed for the rest of his life as 'Dear Colonel Smith'. Had he attained the rank of General he might (or might not) now prefer 'Dear General Smith' to 'Dear Lord Smith'. If his title were not inherited but conferred for his services to the country he may well feel that there would be no point in having it if he were not to be generally known – and addressed – by it.

Similarly, a young peer serving temporarily in the Forces with the rank of captain, but expected to return to civilian life within a year or two could today be addressed, in a letter sent to his home and on a subject unconnected with his service life, as 'Dear Lord Smith' although he should still be addressed as 'Dear Captain Smith' on any service matter.

Sir John Smith, whether he is a baronet or a knight, is addressed as 'Dear Sir John' and his wife as 'Dear Lady Smith'. The form 'Lady (Alice) Smith' is never used as a mode of address.

In the Peerage, the order of precedence is as follows: Royal Dukes, Archbishops, Dukes, Marquesses, Earls, Viscounts, Bishops, Barons (and Scots Lords), Peeresses in their own Right, Life Peers, Life Peeresses.

There were separate Peerages of England, of Scotland and of Ireland until 1707, when the Peerage of Great Britain and Ireland was formed; and of Great Britain and Ireland until 1801, when it became the Peerage of the United Kingdom. The peers and peeresses in each degree – i.e. marquesses, earls and viscounts – rank in the following order: those of England, of Scotland, of Great Britain, of Ireland and of the United Kingdom.

Dames are addressed by title and Christian name only – 'Dear Dame Fanny', never 'Dear Dame Smith' or 'Dear Dame Fanny Smith'. Many people make the mistake of supposing that this perfectly correct method of address sounds too familiar when used by someone who is only an acquaintance and not a close friend. Nevertheless, it is quite correct.

The above applies only to women who have themselves been awarded by the sovereign an honour conferring the title of 'Dame' – e.g. a DBE. It does not apply to wives and widows of baronets and knights whose legal title of 'Dame' is nowadays never used except in legal documents or quotations from these, e.g. the publication of their wills.

The custom of addressing peers and peeresses as 'My Lord' or 'My Lady' has almost entirely gone out of use. For most normal correspondence 'Dear Sir' or 'Dear Madam' is sufficiently formal.

A (British peerage) baron or baroness is addressed by name as 'Dear Lord Smith' or 'Dear Lady Smith' – never 'Dear Baron (or Baroness) Smith'.

The same rule applies to (British) viscounts (and viscountesses), earls (and countesses) and marquesses (and marchionesses). No distinction in this respect is made between inherited and life peerages. If, however, the wife of a peer possessed a courtesy title before her marriage she retains this, if her father's rank was higher than that of her husband. E.g. Miss Jones, on marrying Baron Smith, becomes Lady Smith and should be addressed in this way; but Lady Mary Jones, being the daughter of a Duke or Earl, on marrying Baron Smith becomes Lady Mary Smith and should be addressed as 'Dear Lady Mary'.

There was a time when the question of how to address a peer in an informal business letter would never have arisen because peers were unlikely to receive any business letters at all except from those who were (conventionally) regarded as their inferiors and so bound to address them formally. This no longer applies in an age when many peers are themselves in business, some in quite subordinate positions.

You would address a peer as 'Dear Lord Smith' in cases in which, had he been a commoner, you would have used the form 'Dear Mr Smith'. You would address a peer as 'Dear Smith' only if you were on such terms with him that you would address him as 'Smith' in conversation.

There is no equivalent informal manner of addressing a

peeress, who must be addressed as 'Lady Smith' by those not on Christian name terms. One or two peeresses in their own right have favoured the use of their names without a prefix but this is, so far, a personal idiosyncrasy. Both peers and peeresses (in their own right) use the title name only as a signature, e.g. 'Smith' or 'Exton'; it does not by any means follow that they wish to be addressed in the same way.

In a social letter, a person who was well acquainted with a Duke (though not on Christian name terms) would write 'Dear Duke' unless he were presumed to be a social equal in which case he would write 'Dear Middlesex' using simply the name of the county or place from which the duke took his title. Presumably this manner of address will eventually pass into business use as well, and indeed in a few cases it has already done so. There are, however, very few dukes, and the problem of deciding how to address any of them in other than a formal manner rarely arises.

The one definite rule is that a duke must not be addressed as 'Dear Duke of . . . . . .'.

Courtesy titles

The courtesy title 'Honourable', borne by the sons, daughters and daughters-in-law of viscounts and barons, and the younger sons of earls, is not used in the form of address. The Honourable John or Jane Smith is addressed simply as 'Dear Mr (or Mrs or Miss) Smith'.

The eldest son of an earl, entitled by courtesy to use his father's second title of Viscount, is addressed in the same way as any other Viscount – 'Dear Lord Blank'. His wife, if she has no higher title of her own, is 'Dear Lady Blank'.

In the same way a marquess's eldest son, taking the courtesy title of Earl of Blank (his father's second title), and the eldest son of a duke, by courtesy the Marquess of Blank (his father's second title), are addressed as though they held these titles in their own right. When addressed as 'Lord . . . . . .' they use the territorial, not the family, name – i.e. Lord 'Exton' not Lord 'Smith'.

The courtesy titles which cause most confusion and are most often wrongly used in correspondence as in conversation are those given to the younger sons of dukes and marquesses, and to all the daughters of dukes, marquesses and earls.

This title consists of Lord (or Lady) followed by the first Christian name only and the family surname (not the father's title name), e.g. the younger son of John Smith, Duke of Exshire, is Lord George Smith and his sister is Lady Mary Smith. When Lord John Smith marries, his wife becomes Lady John Smith. If Lady Mary Smith marries plain Mr Jones or Sir John Jones, she keeps her courtesy title while taking her husband's surname, i.e. Lady Mary Jones.

When addressed by name in letters, Lord John Smith must be 'Dear Lord John', his wife must be 'Dear Lady John' while Lady Mary Smith is 'Dear Lady Mary'.

Many people are unaccustomed to meeting with these last titles and consequently feel that the use of the title and Christian name without surname sounds too familiar, while the use of a man's surname in addressing a woman seems odd. As a result holders of these courtesy titles are often wrongly addressed both in speech and by letter as 'Lord (or Lady) Smith (or Jones)'.

Ecclesiastical titles

In addressing those with ecclesiastical titles below the rank of Bishop, the forms 'Dear Rev. Sir' or 'Very Rev. Sir' (for a Dean) or 'Venerable Sir' (for an Archdeacon) are little used today except by some tradesmen with a large clerical clientele. 'Dear Sir' suffices where the correspondent is not to be addressed by name. If the name is used, the form should be 'Dear Mr Blank' or in the case of a Roman Catholic priest or Anglican who elects to use this title, 'Dear Father Blank'. Similarly for holders of doctorates or those of higher ecclesiastical rank, 'Dear Doctor (or Canon or Archdeacon or Monsignor) Blank'.

The old fulsome preambles for bishops and higher ranks are no longer used except in formal ecclesiastical documents. The modern forms of address, formal and less formal respectively, are:

'Bishop': 'My Lord, My Lord Bishop', or 'Dear Bishop Blank' (using his surname, not the name of his see)

'Archbishop': 'My Lord Archbishop' (or more usually nowadays, 'Your Grace'), or 'Dear Archbishop Blank'

'Cardinal': 'My Lord Cardinal', or 'Dear Cardinal Blank'

Titles derived from appointments

There is no special form of address for the Prime Minister and members of the Ministry. The form 'Dear Prime Minister' is not used in business correspondence but only in letters from colleagues or friends.

Ambassadors are addressed as 'Your Excellency' (formal); or 'Dear Mr Smith' or 'Dear Lord Exton'.

The title 'Lord Mayor' is restricted to the chief citizens of some large towns including: London, Birmingham, Liverpool, Manchester, Sheffield, Leeds, Bristol, Hull, Newcastle-upon-Tyne, Nottingham, Bradford, York, Coventry, Norwich, Plymouth, Portsmouth, Stoke-on-Trent, Cardiff, Belfast, Dublin, Cork, and certain cities within the Commonwealth. In Scotland the equivalent title is 'Lord Provost' – for Edinburgh, Aberdeen, Dundee and Glasgow. The Scottish equivalent of Mayor is 'Provost'.

Certain officials are entitled to be styled 'Right Honourable' (usually abbreviated to 'Rt. Hon.') even when not addressed by name. These include:

'The Rt. Hon. the Lord Advocate'
'The Rt. Hon. the Lord High Chancellor'
'The Rt. Hon. the Lord Chief Justice of England'

A Privy Councillor is entitled to the same prefix, with the letters 'PC' following his name, e.g.

'The Rt. Hon. John Smith, PC'

A Lord Mayor of London, York, Belfast, Dublin, Cork and of certain Commonwealth capitals (including Sydney, Melbourne, Adelaide, Perth, Brisbane and Hobart) is also addressed as:

'The Rt. Hon. the Lord Mayor of ......'

The chief citizens of Edinburgh and Glasgow are similarly:

'The Rt. Hon. the Lord Provost of . . . . . .'

Other Lord Mayors or Lord Provosts are addressed as:

'The Lord Mayor . . . . . .' or 'The Lord Provost of . . . . .'

Mayors of cities are:

'The Right Worshipful Mayor of . . . . . .'

Mayors of Boroughs are:

'The Worshipful Mayor of . . . . . .'

An Alderman is addressed as 'Mr Alderman Smith'; or, if titled, 'Alderman Sir John Smith', etc.

Superscriptions

The superscription is the name and address as you put it on the envelope.

Doctors, of any faculty and either sex, are addressed as 'Doctor', with the exception of surgeons and medical men and women of consultant status who are addressed as 'Esq.', 'Mrs' or 'Miss'. In the case of those normally addressed (in conversation) as 'doctor', the superscription 'Doctor John Smith', previously regarded as too informal for business use, is now becoming so usual as to be generally accepted.

A professor who is also a doctor is given the superscription 'Professor John Smith'; or (if he has a knighthood) 'Professor Sir John Smith, KBE' (or whatever the order of his knighthood is); or (if he is a baronet) 'Professor Sir John Smith, Bart'.

Each of the five Lord Justices of Appeal is addressed formally as 'My Lord', the envelope addressed to any such judge should be headed 'The Rt. Hon. the Lord Justice [Jones]' and on judicial matters he will be addressed as 'His Lordship'.

Judges of the High Court are also addressed on judicial matters as 'My Lord' while the envelope should be addressed to: 'The Hon. Mr Justice [Jones]'. 'My Lord' or 'Your Lordship' is the verbal address on judicial matters.

High Court Judges are knighted on appointment while a lady judge on appointment is created a Dame. 'Madam' is the correct beginning for a letter, and the envelope should be addressed to 'The Hon. Mrs Justice [Jones]'. 'Madam' is the formal method of verbal address, or 'Your Ladyship' on judicial matters.

A County Court Judge should be addressed at the start of a letter as 'Sir' – or 'Madam' – and the envelope should be addressed to 'His' – or 'Her' – Honour Judge [Jones]'. 'QC' should be written after the name and he or she will be addressed verbally as 'Your Honour'.

In Scotland a Judge of the College of Justice is given a judicial title on taking his seat on the bench and is known as a Lord of Session. He should be addressed at the beginning of a letter as 'My Lord' and the envelope should be addressed to 'The Hon. Lord [Roberts]'.

A Justice of the Peace, although addressed as 'Your Worship' when on the Bench, is addressed on an envelope merely as:

'John Smith, Esq. (or Miss Mary Smith)' followed by 'JP'.

The superscription for an Ambassador should include both rank and name, the diplomatic rank standing before all others, including royal titles, e.g.

For a British Ambassador:

'His Excellency (Admiral Sir) John Smith, HBM (standing for Her (or His) Britannic Majesty's) Ambassador to ......'

For a foreign Ambassador:

'His Excellency Prince' (or Count or whatever the title may be) followed by the name.

The wife of a British ambassador is usually given the courtesy title of 'Her Excellency' in the country to which her husband is accredited, although not in Britain. Similarly it is customary to address as 'Her Excellency' the wife of a foreign ambassador accredited to the Court of St James's.

Ministers (heads of diplomatic missions which have not been

raised to the status of an embassy) are not entitled to the rank of Excellency and are addressed by their normal style as 'John Smith, Esq.' followed by (in the case of a British Minister) 'HBM Minister Plenipotentiary to ......'

Consuls, of all ranks, are similarly addressed as: 'John Smith, Esq., HBM Consul in ......'

The form 'HBM' instead of the more familiar 'HM' is used because in a foreign country the words 'His (or Her) Majesty' would not necessarily refer to the British monarch.

No rank should be included in the superscription for letters addressed to senior NCOs (CSM upwards) or junior commissioned officers (up to, and including, sub-lieutenant in the Royal Navy, lieutenant in the Army, and pilot officer in the RAF). These are addressed by their civilian titles with an indication of their service following the name, e.g.

> 'John Smith, Esq., RN'
> 'Sir John Smith, KOYLI'
> 'Hon. John Smith, RE'
> 'Lord John Smith, RAF'
> 'Miss Joan Smith, WRAF'

For officers of higher ranks the service rank is included in the name and comes before any civilian title, e.g.

> 'Captain the Earl of Exton, RN'
> 'Colonel Sir John Smith, RE'
> 'Air Vice Marshal the Hon. John Smith, RAF'
> 'Brigadier Joan Smith, WRAC'

While most clergy today welcome, as a sign of their better relationship with the laity, the disuse of the old highly ceremonial forms of address, the correct superscriptions should still be used.

For Anglican clergy the forms are:

> Clergy of the lowest rank:
> 'The Rev. John Smith'

The word 'Reverend' precedes any temporal title, e.g.

'The Rev. Lord John Smith'
'The Rev. Hon. John Smith' (not 'The Rev. and Hon.')

The Christian name, or initials, should always be included. If this is not known and cannot be ascertained, a blank must be left, e.g.

'The Rev. – Smith'

A canon or prebendary is addressed in the same way except that this title takes the place of the Christian name or initial:

'The Rev. Canon Smith'
'The Rev. Prebendary Smith'

The superscription for a Dean is:

'The Very Rev. Dean of Exton'

for an Archdeacon:

'The Venerable the Archdeacon of Exton'
or 'The Venerable John Smith'

and for a Bishop:

'The Right Rev. the Lord Bishop of Exton':

This is also correct for Suffragan bishops.
A retired bishop is addressed as:

'The Right Rev. Bishop Smith',

which is also the correct form for bishops of the Episcopal Church in Scotland as these do not use the territorial title.
The superscription for an Archbishop is:

'His Grace the Lord Archbishop of Exton' or, if retired: 'The Most Rev. Archbishop Smith'.

For Roman Catholic clergy the forms are:

'Cardinal': 'His Eminence Cardinal John Smith' or, if also an 'Archbishop': 'His Eminence Cardinal John Smith, Archbishop of Exton' or 'His Eminence the Cardinal Archbishop of Exton'.

'Archbishop': 'The Most Rev. Archbishop of Exton'
'Bishop': 'The Rt. Rev. the Bishop of Exton'
'Monsignor': according to rank either 'The Right Rev.
Mgr. John Smith (higher) or 'The Very Rev. Mgr. John Smith'
(lower).

'Canon': 'The Very Rev. Canon Smith'; or, if also a
Monsignor: 'The Right Rev. (or Very Rev.) Mgr. Canon Smith'.

For priests of lower rank (secular): 'The Rev. John Smith'.
Those in religious orders have initials of their order after
their name: 'Rev. John Smith, SJ', or 'Rev. John Smith, OP'.
The 'Moderator' of the Church of Scotland is addressed as
'The Right Rev. John Smith' while in office and 'The Very Rev.
John Smith' when he has relinquished office.
The correct superscription for 'Sir John Smith' will depend
on whether he is a baronet, a member of one of the Orders of
Knighthood, or a Knight Bachelor.

'Baronet': 'Sir John Smith, Bart.'
'Knight Bachelor': 'Sir John Smith'
'Knights Grand Cross, Grand Commander, or Commander': as above, but with the appropriate initials after the
name to indicate their Order and rank in it. If they are members
of more than one Order, all the relevant initials must be used
and in the right sequence: 'Sir John Smith, GBE, GCVO,
CMG, OBE'.

The correct form of address (written or verbal) for the wife
or widow of either a knight or a baronet, is 'Lady' followed by
the surname only, e.g. 'Lady Smith'.
However, as one family may contain two or three 'Lady
Smiths', and there may be a dozen others not related to each
other, some distinction has to be made in the superscription, in
order to avoid confusion. This is done as follows:
The wife of a baronet is just 'Lady Smith'. She retains this
title on widowhood unless, or until, the heir is married, when
his wife becomes 'Lady Smith'. Technically she then becomes
'The Dowager Lady Smith' but as few modern women favour
this form, she can be addressed by her Christian name followed

by her late husband's title, which is equally correct, e.g. 'Joan, Lady Smith'.

As a knighthood is not a hereditary title, a knight's widow remains 'Lady Smith'. She is not entitled to the rank of dowager, nor to the dowager's alternative form of address. She may, particularly if her surname is at all a common one, still suffer from the inconvenience of being confused with other 'Lady Smiths'. It is therefore customary for knights' wives, as well as widows, and also for baronets' wives, to adopt the form: 'Lady (Joan) Smith'. This is for use only in the superscription on envelopes, or when compiling lists or otherwise referring to her in writing. The brackets indicate recognition of the fact that she is not entitled to the style of 'Lady Joan Smith', and she should never be addressed by this higher rank, either in a letter or verbally.

'Dukes' are entitled to the form: 'His Grace the Duke of Exton'

'Barons': 'The Right Hon. Lord Exton'
'Viscounts': 'The Right Hon. the Viscount Exton'
'Earls': 'The Right Hon. the Earl of Exton'
'Marquesses': 'The Most Hon. the Marquess of Exton'

The wives of the above are entitled to a similar ceremonial superscription.

Today these forms are rarely used on business letters and the word 'To' can be used instead, often written on the line above the name, e.g.

'To
The Earl of Exton'

Even this is now frequently omitted and the following super-scriptions used:

'Baron': 'Lord Smith' (never 'Baron Smith', except for a foreign title)
'Baron's wife': 'Lady Smith'
'Baroness' in her own right is addressed as such: 'The Baroness Smith'

'Viscount': 'Viscount Smith'
'Viscount's wife' or a 'Viscountess' in her own right: 'The Viscountess Smith'
'Earl': 'The Earl of Exton'
'Earl's wife' or a 'Countess' in her own right: 'The Countess of Exton'
'Marquess': 'The Marquess of Exton'
'Marquess's wife': 'The Marchioness of Exton'
'Duke': 'His Grace the Duke of Exton'

Honours and awards

The superscription should include all honours, awards, academic and other distinctions to which the person is entitled. When addressing anyone who has had a very distinguished career, the simplest way of ensuring that all the letters after his name are included, and in the right order, is to check with an up-to-date book of reference. This, obviously, may not include recent awards. The following rules will help to show in which order additional letters should be included.

The 'VC' (Victoria Cross) takes precedence over all other honours of any kind.

The 'GC' (George Cross) comes before everything except the Victoria Cross.

'KG' (Knight of the Garter) stands next.

'PC' (Privy Councillor) stands before everything except the above. All Cabinet Ministers are Privy Councillors. British Orders of Knighthood follow in their own order of precedence, provided that in each case the award is of the same grade within the order. A higher grade of a junior order comes before a lower grade of a senior order, e.g. 'KCB' (Knight Commander of the Bath) precedes 'KCVO' (Knight Commander of the Royal Victorian Order), but 'KCVO' precedes 'CB' (Commander of the Bath).

The Orders of Chivalry rank as follows: The Most Noble Order of the Garter (KG), The Most Ancient and Most Noble Order of the Thistle (KT), The Most Illustrious Order of Saint Patrick (KP), The Most Honourable Order of the Bath (GCB,

KCB or CB), The Order of Merit (OM), The Most Exalted Order of the Star of India (GCSI), The Most Distinguished Order of St Michael and St George (GCMG, KCMG, DCMG or CMG), The Most Eminent Order of the Indian Empire (GCIE, KCIE or CIE), The Royal Victorian Order (GCVO, KCVO, DCVO, CVO, MVO), The Royal Victorian Chain, The Most Excellent Order of the British Empire (GBE, KBE, DBE, CBE, OBE or MBE), Order of the Companions of Honour (CH), The Royal Order of Victoria and Albert (for Ladies) (VA), The Imperial Order of the Crown of India (for Ladies) (CI), The Imperial Service Order (ISO).

It will be seen that the three senior orders – of the Garter, the Thistle and St Patrick – have only one class, that of Knight. Of the rest, most have several classes which include, in descending order a variety of the following: Knight Grand Cross or Knight Grand Commander, Knight Commander, Dame Commander, Commander, Officer, and Member.

Certain high honours awarded by the Sovereign have, however, been interspersed into this older list of precedence in the following manner:

'OM' (Order of Merit) comes immediately after the Knight Grand Cross of the Order of the Bath, i.e. before all lower grades of this order and all grades of lesser orders, such as the Royal Victorian Order and the Order of the British Empire.

'CH' (Companion of Honour) comes immediately after the Knight (or Dame) Grand Cross of the Order of the British Empire.

'DSO' (Distinguished Service Order) comes immediately before the fourth class of the RVO and the OBE (that is, the MVO, OBE and MBE) but after all grades of all other Orders.

'RRC' (Royal Red Cross, awarded to women) comes immediately after the MBE.

Gallantry and Service awards follow in this order:

> 'DSC' (Distinguished Service Cross)
> 'MC' (Military Cross)
> 'DFC' (Distinguished Flying Cross)
> 'AFC' (Air Force Cross)

'DCM' (Distinguished Conduct Medal)
'CGM' (Conspicuous Gallantry Medal)
'GM' (George Medal)
'DSM' (Distinguished Service Medal)
'MM' (Military Medal)
'DFM' (Distinguished Flying Medal)
'AFM' (Air Force Medal)
'BEM' (British Empire Medal)
'VD' (Volunteer Officers' Decoration)
'TD' (Territorial Decoration)
'ED' (Efficiency Decoration)

As all the above are awarded by the Sovereign, the order in which the letters denoting them appear after the holder's name is governed by the order of precedence laid down for the wearing of the respective insignia or medals and ribbons.

There is one other invariable rule. The letters 'MP' (Member of Parliament) always come last, because this is a temporary addition, used only while the holder is representing a constituency.

The normal order is governed by the following customary rules:

'QC' (Queen's Counsel), or 'KC' (during the reign of a King) come before academic qualifications, since they are, at least technically, distinctions derived from the sovereign, e.g. 'Sir John Smith, MC, QC'.

The following highly coveted and rarer royal distinctions usually follow academic degrees and professional qualifications:

'QHC' (Honorary Chaplain to the Queen)
'QHP' (Honorary Physician to the Queen)
'QHS' (Honorary Surgeon to the Queen)
'QHDS' (Honorary Dental Surgeon to the Queen)

Academic degrees are given in rising order of importance, that is, Bachelor, Master, Doctor; e.g. BA, BSc, etc.; MA, MMs, etc.; DPhil, DSc, etc. But only the highest distinction gained in any one faculty is normally used.

Although it is not correct to include academic distinctions

below the grade of doctor (such as BSc or MA) in the super-scription of private letters, these are usually included for the purposes of business correspondence, if their existence is known to the writer. In general, people whose degrees add to their professional status (such as school-masters, medical prac-titioners) set more store on having these included in their superscriptions than do those whose professional careers have been entirely independent of academic distinctions.

Academic degrees are followed by professional qualifications, and abbreviations denoting 'Fellows', 'Licentiates' and 'Mem-bers' of professional bodies. As far as these last are concerned there is no order of preferences sufficiently generally used by their holders to be regarded as even customary. Some people opt for descending order of importance as with 'honours', others choose rising order and put fellowships last, some place distinc-tions awarded by senior bodies before those awarded by newer bodies, and some follow the order in which the distinctions were obtained, simply adding on any additional qualifications as these come along, e.g. 'MRCS, LRCP (Member of the Royal College of Surgeons, and Licentiate of the Royal College of Physicians) or 'LRCP, MRCS'. Whatever the order, only the highest grade of membership of any professional body is included, e.g. 'MRCS' is discarded once the holder becomes an 'FRCS' (Fellow).

'JP' (Justice of the Peace) follows such professional quali-fications, immediately preceding MP.

9 Abbreviations

There are enough abbreviations in common use to fill a book as large as the one you are reading. Some are normally used only by specialists, some are Service abbreviations, and others are the abbreviations which are common in business letters but which you are unlikely to see elsewhere. Here are a few of the most usual ones. As you will see, some abbreviations consisting of two or three letters mean one thing if they are written in capitals and something different if they are written in lower case.

A Army; Associate; Association.
AA anti-aircraft; Automobile Association.
AACCA Associate of the Association of Certified and Corporate Accountants.
AB Able-bodied Seaman; Assistance Board.
abbr, abbrev abbreviation.
AC Aircraft(s)man; Alternating Current; Assistant Commissioner.
a/c account.
ACA Associate of the Institute of Chartered Accountants.
acct account; accountant.
ACII Associate of the Chartered Insurance Institute.
ACIS Associate of the Chartered Institute of Secretaries.
ACM Air Chief-Marshal.
add addendum.
AERE Atomic Energy Research Establishment.
AEU Amalgamated Engineering Union.
AFA Amateur Football Association; Associate of the Faculty of Actuaries.

AFAS Associate of the Faculty of Architects and Surveyors.
AFC Air Force Cross.
AFM Air Force Medal.
AFS Associate of the Faculty of Secretaries.
AIC Associate of the Institute of Chemistry.
AICE Associate of the Institute of Civil Engineers.
AIL Associate of the Institute of Linguists.
AIMechE Associate of the Institution of Mechanical
    Engineers.
AIMinE Associate of the Institution of Mining Engineers.
AISA Associate of the Incorporated Secretaries' Association.
ALA Associate of the Library Association.
AMC Association of Municipal Corporations.
AMICE Associate Member of the Institution of Civil
    Engineers.
AMIChemE Associate Member of the Institute of Chemical
    Engineers.
AMIEE Associate Member of the Institution of Electrical
    Engineers.
AMIMechE Associate Member of the Institution of
    Mechanical Engineers.
AMIMinE Associate Member of the Institution of Mining
    Engineers.
AMIRE Associate Member of the Institution of Radio
    Engineers.
AMIStructE Associate Member of the Institution of
    Structural Engineers.
anon anonymous.
APS Associate of the Pharmaceutical Society.
ARA Associate of the Royal Academy.
ARAD Associate of the Royal Academy of Dancing.
ARAeS Associate of the Royal Aeronautical Society.
ARAM Associate of the Royal Academy of Music.
ARCM Associate of the Royal College of Music.
ARCO Associate of the Royal College of Organists.
ARCS Associate of the Royal College of Science.
ARIBA Associate of the Royal Institute of British Architects.

ARSA Associate of the Royal Scottish Academy; Associate of the Royal Society of Arts.

ARWS Associate of the Royal Society of Painters in Water Colours.

ASAA Associate of the Society of Incorporated Accountants and Auditors.

ASE Amalgamated Society of Engineers.

ASLEF Amalgamated Society of Locomotive Engineers and Firemen.

AU Angström Unit.

AVM Air Vice-Marshal.

BA Bachelor of Arts; British Academy; British Association.

BAgr(ic) Bachelor of Agriculture.

BCh Bachelor of Surgery (L. *Baccalaureus Chirurgiae*).

BChD Bachelor of Dental Surgery.

BCL Bachelor of Civil Law.

BComm Bachelor of Commerce.

BD Bachelor of Divinity.

BDS Bachelor of Dental Surgery.

BEd Bachelor of Education.

BEM British Empire Medal.

BEng Bachelor of Engineering

bf brought forward.

BIM British Institute of Management.

BL Bachelor of Law; Bachelor of Letters; British Legion; bill of lading.

BLitt Bachelor of Letters (L. *Baccalaureus Literarum*).

BM Bachelor of Medicine; British Museum; Brigade-Major.

BMA British Medical Association.

BMus Bachelor of Music.

BPhil Bachelor of Philosophy.

BRCS British Red Cross Society.

BS British Standard; Bachelor of Surgery; bill of sale.

BSc Bachelor of Science.

BSI British Standards Institution.

C centigrade; Cape; Central; 100.

c.   cent; centigram; centimetre; century; chapter; about
(L. *circa*).

CA   Chartered Accountant; Consumers' Association.

CAB   Citizens' Advice Bureau.

CB   Companion of (the Order of) the Bath; County Borough.

CBE   Commander of (the Order of) the British Empire.

CC   County Council; Cricket Club.

cc   cubic centimetre.

cd   with dividend (L. *cum* — 'with').

cf   compare (L. *confer*).

cfi   cost, freight and insurance.

CGM   Conspicuous Gallantry Medal.

CH   Companion of Honour.

ChB   Bachelor of Surgery (L. *Chirurgiae Baccalaureus*).

ChM   Master of Surgery (L. *Chirurgiae Magister*).

CID   Criminal Investigation Department.

CIE   Companion of (the Order of) the Indian Empire.

cif   cost, insurance and freight.

CIGS   Chief of the Imperial General Staff.

C-in-C   Commander-in-Chief.

CM   Master of Surgery (L. *Chirurgiae Magister*); Certificated
Master; Corresponding Member.

cm   centimetre.

CMG   Companion of the Order of St Michael and St George.

CO   Commanding Officer; conscientious objector.

Co   County; Company.

c/o   care of.

COD   cash on delivery.

Cons   Conservative; Consul.

cos   cosine.

cosec   cosecant.

cot   cotangent.

CPS   Keeper of the Privy Seal (L. *Custos Privati Sigilli*).

CR   Keeper of the Rolls (L. *Custos Rotulorum*).

cr   credit; creditor.

CSI   Companion of (the Order of) the Star of India.

CSM   Company Sergeant-Major.

ct   carat; cent.

CVO Commander of the (Royal) Victorian Order.

CWO cash with order.

CWS Co-operative Wholesale Society.

cwt hundredweight.

d date; day; died; diameter.

DA days of acceptance; deposit account; Diploma of Art; District Attorney.

db decibel.

DBE Dame Commander of (the Order of) the British Empire.

DC District of Columbia; District Court; Direct Current.

DCL Doctor of Civil Law.

DCM Distinguished Conduct Medal.

DCMG Dame Commander of the Order of St Michael and St George.

DCVO Dame Commander of the Royal Victorian Order.

DD Doctor of Divinity.

DDS Doctor of Dental Surgery.

dec declination; decorated.

decd deceased.

del delegate; delete.

DF Defender of the Faith; Dean of the Faculty.

DFC Distinguished Flying Cross.

DFM Distinguished Flying Medal.

DG by the grace of God (L. *Dei gratia*); thanks be to God (*Deo gratias*).

DLitt Doctor of Letters.

dm decimetre.

DMus Doctor of Music.

do ditto, the same.

Dom Lord, Master (L. *Dominus*); Dominion.

DOMS Diploma in Ophthalmic Medicine and Surgery.

doz dozen.

DPH Diploma of Public Health.

DPhil Doctor of Philosophy.

DQMG Deputy Quartermaster-General.

Dr Doctor; debtor.

dr dram; (Banking) drawer.

D/s, ds   days after sight.
DSc   Doctor of Science.
DSC   Distinguished Service Cross.
DSM   Distinguished Service Medal.
DSO   Distinguished Service Order.
dsp   died without issue (L. *decessit sine prole*).
DTh   Doctor of Theology.
DV   God willing (L. *Deo volente*).

E   East; Eastern.
E and OE   errors and omissions excepted.
EC   East Central; Established Church; Education Committee.
EE   Envoy Extraordinary; errors excepted.
ejusd   of the same (L. *ejusdem*).
emf   electro-motive force.
eq   equal; equivalent.
ER   Queen Elizabeth (L. *Elizabeth Regina*).
ESP   extra-sensory perception.
et al   and others (L. *et alia*); and elsewhere (L. *et alibi*).
et seq   and the following (L. *et sequentia*).
ETU   Electrical Trades Union.
Exc   Excellency.
exc   except; exception.
exr, exor   executor.

F   Fahrenheit; Father; Fellow.
f   farthing; fathom; folio.
FA   Football Association; Fine Arts.
FACCA   Fellow of the Association of Certified and Corporate
   Accountants.
FAI   Fellow of the (Chartered) Auctioneers' and Estate Agents'
   Institute.
FAS   Fellow of the Antiquarian Society; Fellow of the
   Anthropological Society.
FBA   Fellow of the British Academy; Fellow of the British
   Association.
FBI   Federal Bureau of Investigation (US).
FBOA   Fellow of the British Optical Association.
FCP   Fellow of the College of Preceptors.

FD Defender of the Faith (L. *Fidei Defensor*).

fec made by (L. *fecit*).

FEIS Fellow of the Educational Institute of Scotland.

ff following (pages); folios.

FFA Fellow of the Faculty of Actuaries.

FGS Fellow of the Geological Society.

FIA Fellow of the Institute of Actuaries.

FIAC Fellow of the Institute of Company Accountants.

FIAS Fellow (Surveyor Member) of the Incorporated
     Association of Architects and Surveyors.

Fid Def Defender of the Faith (L. *Fidei Defensor*).

FIJ Fellow of the Institute of Journalists.

FIL Fellow of the Institute of Linguists.

fin at the end (L. *finis*); financial.

FISA Fellow of the Incorporated Secretaries' Association.

FISE Fellow of the Institution of Sanitary Engineers.

FLA Fellow of the Library Association.

Flt-Lt Flight-Lieutenant.

FM Field-Marshal; frequency modulation.

FO Flying Officer; Foreign Office.

fo firm offer; folio.

fob free on board.

fp foot-pound.

FRAM Fellow of the Royal Academy of Music.

FRAS Fellow of the Royal Astronomical Society; Fellow of
     the Royal Asiatic Society.

FRBS Fellow of the Royal Society of British Sculptors.

FRCM Fellow of the Royal College of Music.

FRCO Fellow of the Royal College of Organists.

FRCP Fellow of the Royal College of Physicians.

FRCS Fellow of the Royal College of Surgeons.

FRCVS Fellow of the Royal College of Veterinary Surgeons.

FRGS Fellow of the Royal Geographical Society.

FRHS Fellow of the Royal Horticultural Society.

FRHist-Soc Fellow of the Royal Historical Society.

FRIBA Fellow of the Royal Institute of British Architects.

FRIC Fellow of the Royal Institute of Chemistry.

FRICS Fellow of the Royal Institution of Chartered Surveyors.

FRMetS   Fellow of the Royal Meteorological Society.
FRPS   Fellow of the Royal Faculty of Physicians and
    Surgeons.
FRS   Fellow of the Royal Society.
FRSA   Fellow of the Royal Society of Arts.
FRSE   Fellow of the Royal Society of Edinburgh.
FRSGS   Fellow of the Royal Scottish Geographical Society.
FRSL   Fellow of the Royal Society of Literature.
FRSSA   Fellow of the Royal Scottish Society of Arts.
FSA   Fellow of the Society of Antiquaries.
FSAA   Fellow of the Society of Incorporated Accountants and
    Auditors.
FSE   Fellow of the Society of Engineers.
FSS   Fellow of the Royal Statistical Society.
ft   foot, feet; fort; fortification.
fur   furlong.
fv   on the back of the page (L. *folio verso*).
FZS   Fellow of the Zoological Society of London.

g   gauge; genitive; gramme; guinea.
gal   gallon(s).
GATT   General Agreement on Tariffs and Trade.
GBE   Knight/Dame Grand Cross of (the Order of) the British
    Empire.
GC   George Cross.
GCB   Knight Grand Cross of (the Order of) the Bath.
GCIE   Knight Grand Commander of (the Order of) the
    Indian Empire.
GCMG   Knight Grand Cross of (the Order of) St Michael
    and St George.
GCSI   Knight Grand Commander of (the Order of) the Star of
    India.
GCVO   Knight/Dame Grand Cross of the (Royal) Victorian
    Order.
GHQ   General Headquarters.
GI   government issue; US private soldier.
GLC   Greater London Council.

gm   gramme.
GM   George Medal.
GMT   Greenwich Mean Time.
GP   general practitioner.

h and c   hot and cold (water).
HB   hard black (of a lead pencil).
HBM   Her (His) Britannic Majesty.
hcf   highest common factor.
HE   high-explosive; His Eminence; His Excellency.
HF   high frequency.
HH   His (Her) Highness; His Holiness (the Pope).
HIH   His (Her) Imperial Highness.
HM   Her (His) Majesty.
HMS   Her (His) Majesty's Service; Her (His) Majesty's Ship.
HMSO   Her (His) Majesty's Stationery Office.
Hon   Honorary; Honourable.
Hon Sec   Honorary Secretary.
hp   hire purchase; horse power.
HQ   headquarters.
HRH   His (Her) Royal Highness.
HSH   His (Her) Serene Highness.
HT   high tension.

ib, ibid   in the same place (L. *ibidem*).
i/c   in charge of.
ICA   Institute of Chartered Accountants.
id   the same (L. *idem*).
ie   that is, namely (L. *id est*).
IF   intermediate frequency.
ILO   International Labour Organisation.
IMF   International Monetary Fund.
Imp   Emperor (L. *imperator*); imperial.
imp   imperfect; imperative; imported.
in   inch, inches.
Inc, Incorp   Incorporated.
incog   unknown (L. *incognito*).
inf   below (L. *infra*); infinitive.
init   at the beginning (L. *initio*).

INRI Jesus of Nazareth, King of the Jews (L. *Jesus Nazarenus Rex Judaeorum*).
Inst Institute.
InstCE Institution of Civil Engineers.
InstEE Institution of Electrical Engineers.
in trans in transit.
inv he designed/invented it.
IOW Isle of Wight.
IQ intelligence quotient.
IWGC Imperial War Graves Commission.

JCD Doctor of Civil Law (L. *Juris Civilis Doctor*); Doctor of Canon Law (L. *Juris Canonici Doctor*).
JD Doctor of Laws (L. *Jurum Doctor*).
JP Justice of the Peace.
jr junior.
JUD Doctor of both (Civil and Canon) Laws (L. *Juris utriusque Doctor*).

K King; Knight.
KBE Knight Commander of (the Order of) the British Empire.
KC King's Counsel.
KCB Knight Commander of (the Order of) the Bath.
KCIE Knight Commander of (the Order of) the Indian Empire.
KCMG Knight Commander of (the Order of) St Michael and St George.
KCSI Knight Commander of (the Order of) the Star of India.
KCVO Knight Commander of the (Royal) Victorian Order.
KG Knight of the Garter.
kg kilogram(s).
km kilometre(s).
KP Knight of St Patrick.
Kt Knight.
KT Knight of the Order of the Thistle.
kw kilowatt.

L   Latin
l   latitude, left; line.
Lab   Labrador; Labour.
lb   pound (L. *libra*).
LCP   Licentiate of the College of Preceptors.
LDS   Licentiate of Dental Surgery.
L/F, lf   low frequency.
LFAS   Licentiate of the Faculty of Architects and Surveyors.
LFPS   Licentiate of the Faculty of Physicians and Surgeons.
lhd   left hand drive.
LittD   Doctor of Letters.
LLB   Bachelor of Laws (L. *Legum Baccalaureus*).
LLCM   Licentiate of the London College of Music.
LLD   Doctor of Laws (L. *Legum Doctor*).
LLM   Master of Laws (L. *Legum Magister*).
loc cit   in the place cited (L. *loco citato*).
log   logarithm.
loq   he speaks (L. *loquitur*).
LP   Labour Party; Letters Patent; long-playing (record).
LPTB   London Passenger Transport Board.
LRAM   Licentiate of the Royal Academy of Music.
LRCM   Licentiate of the Royal College of Medicine.
LRCP   Licentiate of the Royal College of Physicians.
LRCS   Licentiate of the Royal College of Surgeons.
LRCVS   Licentiate of the Royal College of Veterinary
   Surgeons.
LRIBA   Licentiate of the Royal Institute of British Architects.
LSA   Licentiate of the Society of Apothecaries.
lt   low tension; long ton.
Lt   Lieutenant.
Lt-Cdr   Lieutenant-Commander.
Lt-Col   Lieutenant-Colonel.
Lt-Gen   Lieutenant-General.
Ltd   Limited.

M   Majesty; Marshal; Master; 1000.
m   married; masculine; mass; medium; metre; mile; minute.
MA   Master of Arts.

MB   Bachelor of Medicine (L. *Medicinae Baccalaureus*).

MBE   Member of (the Order of) the British Empire.

MC   Military Cross.

MCC   Marylebone Cricket Club.

MCh   Master of Surgery (L. *Magister Chirurgiae*).

MComm   Master of Commerce (and Administration).

MCPS   Member of the (Royal) College of Physicians and Surgeons; megacycles per second.

MD   Doctor of Medicine (L. *Medicinae Doctor*); mentally deficient.

MEd   Master of Education.

mem   remember (L. *memento*).

mfr   manufacturer.

mg   milligram.

Mgr   Monsignor.

MICE   Member of the Institution of Civil Engineers.

MIEE   Member of the Institution of Electrical Engineers.

MIMechE   Member of the Institution of Mechanical Engineers.

MM   Military Medal.

mm   millimetre.

MMB   Milk Marketing Board.

MO   Medical Officer; Money Order.

MOH   Medical Officer of Health.

MP   Member of Parliament; Metropolitan Police; Military Police.

mph   miles per hour.

MS   Master of Surgery.

MS(S)   manuscript(s).

MSc   Master of Science.

MusB(ac)   Bachelor of Music.

MusD(oc)   Doctor of Music.

MVO   Member of the (Royal) Victorian Order.

N   North(ern); New; National.

n   name; noun; born (L. *natus*).

n/a, na   no account.

NAAFI   Navy, Army and Air Force Institutes.

NALGO   National and Local Government Officers' Association.
NATO   North Atlantic Treaty Organisation.
NB   note well (L. *nota bene*); North Britain; North British.
NCB   National Coal Board.
NCO   Non-commissioned Officer.
nd   no date.
NE   North-East(ern).
nem con   no one contradicting (L. *nemine contradicente*).
nem dis(s)   no one dissenting (L. *nemine dissentiente*).
NFBTO   National Federation of Building Trades Operatives.
NFU   National Farmers' Union.
non seq   it does not follow (L. *non sequitur*).
No(s)   number(s) (L. *numero*).
NP   Notary Public.
ns   not specified; not sufficient.
NSPCC   National Society for the Prevention of Cruelty to Children.
NUPBP   National Union of Printing, Bookbinding and Paper Workers.
NUR   National Union of Railwaymen.
NUS   National Union of Seamen; National Union of Students.
NUT   National Union of Teachers.

o/a   on account of.
ob   he/she died.
OBE   Officer of (the Order of) the British Empire.
o/c   overcharge.
OECD   Organisation for Economic Co-operation and Development.
OM   Order of Merit.
op   a work (L. *opus*).
op cit   in the work quoted (L. *opere citato*).
oz   ounce(s).

p   page; pint.
PA   Press Association.
pa   by the year (L. *per annum*).

par paragraph; parallel; parish.
PAYE Pay As You Earn (Tax).
PC Privy Councillor; Police Constable; Parish Council.
pc per cent; post card.
pd paid.
PhD Doctor of Philosophy.
PM Prime Minister; Provost Marshal.
pm afternoon (L. *post meridiem*); after death (L. *post mortem*).
PMG Postmaster-General; Paymaster General.
PO Petty Officer; Pilot Officer; Postal Order; Post Office.
POW Prisoner of War.
pp on behalf of, by proxy (L. *per procurationem*); post paid.
pp pages.
PPS additional postscript (L. *post postscriptum*).
PRO Public Relations Officer.
PS postscript.
Pte (Army) Private.
PTO Please turn over.

Q Queen; quart(s); question.
QB Queen's Bench.
QC Queen's Counsel.
qed which was to be proved (L. *quod erat demonstrandum*).
qu query; question; as if (L. *quasi*).
qv which see (L. *quod vide*).

RA Royal Academician; Royal Artillery.
RAC Royal Armoured Corps; Royal Automobile Club.
RADA Royal Academy of Dramatic Art.
RADC Royal Army Dental Corps.
RAEC Royal Army Educational Corps.
RAF Royal Air Force.
RAM Royal Academy of Music.
RAMC Royal Army Medical Corps.
RAOC Royal Army Ordnance Corps.
RAPC Royal Army Pay Corps.
RAVC Royal Army Veterinary Corps.
RCA Royal College of Art.
RCM Royal College of Music.

RCP Royal College of Physicians; Royal College of Preceptors.
RCS Royal College of Surgeons; Royal Corps of Signals.
RCVS Royal College of Veterinary Surgeons.
R/D (Banking) refer to drawer.
RE Royal Engineers.
Rear-Adm Rear-Admiral.
ref reference.
Reg Queen (L. *regina*); registered.
Reg Prof Regius Professor.
REME Royal Electrical and Mechanical Engineers.
retd retired; returned; retained.
RF, rf radio frequency.
RGS Royal Geographical Society.
RHistSoc Royal Historical Society.
RHS Royal Horticultural Society.
RIBA Royal Institute of British Architects.
RICS Royal Institution of Chartered Surveyors.
RIP may he/she rest in peace (L. *requiescat in pace*).
RIPH Royal Institute of Public Health.
RM Royal Mail; Royal Marines.
RMP Royal Military Police.
RN Royal Navy.
RNR Royal Naval Reserve.
RNVR Royal Naval Volunteer Reserve.
rpm revolutions per minute.
rps revolutions per second.
RR Right Reverend.
RSA Royal Scottish Academician; Royal Society of Arts;
  Royal Society of Antiquaries.
RSAM Royal Scottish Academy of Music.
RSM Regimental Sergeant-Major; Royal School of Mines;
  Royal Society of Medicine.
RSPCA Royal Society for the Prevention of Cruelty to
  Animals.
RSVP Please Reply (French: *Répondez s'il vous plaît*).
RT Radio-Telegraphy.
RWS Royal Society of Painters in Water Colours.
S South; Scottish; Society; Socialist.

s   second; shilling; son; singular.
sae   stamped addressed envelope.
ScB   Bachelor of Science (L. *Scientiae Baccalaureus*).
ScD   Doctor of Science (L. *Scientiae Doctor*).
SEATO   South-East Asia Treaty Organisation.
Sec   secondary; section; secretary.
sec leg   according to law (L. *secundum legem*).
seq   the following (L. *sequentia*).
sg   specific gravity.
Sgt   Sergeant.
sin   (Mathematics) sine.
SJAA   St John Ambulance Association.
SNP   Scottish Nationalist Party.
SOS   signal of distress.
SPCK   Society for Promoting Christian Knowledge.
Sr   Senior; Sir; Sister.
SRN   State Registered Nurse.
SS   steamship; Straits Settlements.
St   Saint; Street; Strait.
SWG   Standard Wire Gauge.

TA   Territorial Army.
tan   (Mathematics) tangent.
TASS   News Agency of the Soviet Union (*Russian Telegrafnoye Agenstvo Sovietskovo Soyuza*).
TB   tuberculosis; Torpedo Boat.
TD   Territorial Decoration (Officer).
Test   testament(ary); testator.
tfer   transfer.
TGWU   Transport and General Workers' Union.
TNT   high-explosive (trinitrotoluene).
TT   total abstainer (i.e. teetotaller; Tourist Trophy; tuberculin tested.
TU   Trade Union; Transmission Unit.
TUC   Trades Union Congress.

U   Upper; University; Union(ist).
UDC   Urban District Council.
UK   United Kingdom.

UN(O)   United Nations (Organisation).
UNAC   United Nations Appeal for Children.
UNCFS   United National Conference on Food and
  Agriculture.
UNESCO   United Nations Educational, Scientific and
  Cultural Organisation.
UNRRA   United Nations Relief and Rehabilitation
  Administration.
US(A)   United States (of America).
USSR   Union of Socialist Soviet Republics.

v   against (L. *versus*); see (L. *vide*); verb; verse; Vice-
  (L. 'in place of'); volume.
VA   Royal Order of Victoria and Albert.
VC   Victoria Cross; Vice-Chancellor.
VD   Volunteer (Officers') Decoration; venereal disease.
VHF   very high frequency.
vid   see (L. *vide*).
viz   namely (L. *videlicet*).
vs   against (L. *versus*).

W   West(ern); Welsh.
w   wife; width; with; wicket.
WC   West Central; Wesleyan Chapel; water closet.
WHO   World Health Organisation.
Wing-Cdr   Wing-Commander.
W/L   wavelength.
WRAC   Women's Royal Army Corps.
WRAF   Women's Royal Air Force.
WRNS   Women's Royal Naval Service.
WRVS   Women's Royal Voluntary Service.
WS   Writer to the Signet; weather ship.
W/T   wireless telegraphy.
wt   weight.

x   (Mathematics) unknown quantity.

YHA   Youth Hostels Association.
YMCA   Young Men's Christian Association.
YWCA   Young Women's Christian Association.

CREATIVE WRITING

DIANNE DOUBTFIRE

A lively and comprehensive handbook packed with practical advice for everyone with the urge to write.

This book looks at every form of writing – articles, short stories, poetry, plays, novels and non-fiction – and the different techniques of writing for adults or children, radio or TV. It offers clear guidelines for developing your talent and acquiring the basic craftsmanship which is the key to success. Dianne Doubtfire – established author, tutor and lecturer in creative writing – shares her experience and expertise to show how, given dedication and determination, you can not only improve your writing, but have the added satisfaction of seeing it in print.

TEACH YOURSELF BOOKS

ENGLISH GRAMMAR

B. A. PHYTHIAN

This book is intended for the general reader who wishes to familiarise himself with the basic elements of English grammar.

There are chapters on the nature and function of all the principal parts of speech and detailed consideration is given to sentence structure through a study of clauses and phrases. A particular feature of the book is that exercises to test and reinforce comprehension of every stage are built in after each section, with further revision exercises at the end of each chapter.

The student who successfully completes this work will have a sound grasp of correct grammar, and an appreciation of the subtlety and variety of English expression.

TEACH YOURSELF BOOKS

GOOD ENGLISH

B. A. PHYTHIAN

This practical guide and reference handbook will help you improve your own use of English in everyday life and enhance your appreciation of good English writing.

The book first provides handy summaries of the main rules of grammar and punctuation. It then examines some of the more common errors in spoken and written English, before giving practical advice on spelling and helpful definitions of words which are frequently confused and misused.

The second half of the book focuses on the correct and effective use of English in a wide variety of contexts, and illustrates the different types of language and style which contribute to the subtlety and variety of English expression. A particularly useful feature of the book is an extensive guide to the conventions of written English in everyday life, including business and commercial English, letters, reports, summaries and précis, and English for examinations.

TEACH YOURSELF BOOKS

SPELLING

PATRICK THORNHILL

An indispensable guide for everyone who has to put pen to paper or paper to typewriter.

This book is essential for all uncertain spellers who want a quick way of finding out how a word should be spelt. The author has devised a unique and simple system based on sounds which quickly guide a mis-speller to the correct spelling of a word and its derivatives.

The vocabulary equals that of a medium-sized dictionary. It includes words in everyday use which have not yet found their way into many dictionaries, American spellings, foreign words and phrases in common use, and also some words that are used mainly in Australia and New Zealand.

TEACH YOURSELF BOOKS